Buonissimo!

Minimum effort, maximum satisfaction

Gino D'Acampo

photography by Kate Whitaker

Kyle Books

To Luciano and Rocco:
The best things I've ever made.

Introduction

I cannot believe that it has been a year since I wrote my first book *Fantastico!* and here I am again writing the introduction to my second one. The first thing I want to do is thank all of you who supported me. *Fantastico!* received the 'Gourmand Cookbook Award' for the Best Italian Cookery Book in the World in 2007, but even more inspiring has been the response to my recipes in that book. I hope you like this one just as much!

So why is this book called *Buonissimo*? Well, it means something that is very tasty, and of course in this case, we are talking about food and Italian food, in particular.

Over the last year, I have spent a lot of time in Italy with students and other chefs, trying to get as much inspiration as possible, and creating easy and tasty recipes for every occasion. Some of the recipes have come from my grandfather's old notes that he left me and I am very proud that I can share them with all of you.

I have tried to write recipes not just from Naples, the town I come from, but also from the other regions of Italy. I have taken traditional recipes and, using my philosophy of keeping things simple and not using too many ingredients, made them my own.

For this book, I also wanted to make sure there are recipes for every occasion. I believe food should play a huge part in our lives, as a celebration, to bring comfort and to seduce, as well as nourish and sustain us. So there are five chapters in this book, which I hope will suit every kind of person, for every type of meal.

If you want to impress somebody, then the recipes in *Romantico* are for you. These are recipes for two people, full of luxurious ingredients, and much more effective than a bunch of flowers. And I think these recipes will also work even if the meal isn't romantic, but a special meal for your mother, best friend or boss.

Per Me are recipes for one person, whether you live alone or when everyone else has gone out and you want a simple, tasty meal just for yourself. Often you can make a big batch and save the rest for another time. On the other hand, *Salute* is the party chapter. Here are finger food recipes for lots of people or posh nosh for a dinner party.

Facile Facile and *Per Tutti I Giorni* are just the opposite. These are chapters for quick and easy recipes which use storecupboard ingredients and provide ideas for comforting family suppers for weekdays. If you make sure you have a good choice of these ingredients to hand, you should be able to make any of these recipes at short notice.

The last thing I want to do is remind you that there is no such thing as a bad cook. You just need to believe in yourself, choose the right ingredients and, of course, use this book! Cooking impressively does not have to be difficult – I promise you, you won't get stressed in my kitchen, but your guests will love you!

And my rules for success: pour yourself a nice glass of wine, throw everyone else out of the kitchen, make sure your ingredients are fresh and of good quality and that your knife is sharp and, finally, only cook if you are in a good mood.

In this book, you will find recipes that are *Buonissimo* and once you have tried them, you will understand my motto:

Minimum effort, maximum satisfaction!

Romantico

Elegant recipes for two

This was, of course, the easiest chapter for me

to write as Italians are born with natural romantic style. I wrote this for all of you who need that little bit of help to show your loved one what they mean to you or for those of you who are trying to catch the girl or boy of your dreams. Apart from choosing the right recipe, getting the wine right is an essential part of a romantic dinner. Make sure that you dress for the occasion, set the scene with the right music and don't forget the most important rule – you are there to spoil your partner. Good luck and if things don't go quite to plan, don't blame the food!

Topolini al Tartufo e Salvia

If you really want to show your partner that you have made lots of effort to prepare a romantic dinner, this is the dish to make. It takes a little more time than the others as you literally prepare it from scratch, but it's so worth it. If you really don't like truffles, leave out the truffle-flavoured olive oil but please make sure that the Parmesan cheese is freshly grated and not the dried rubbish you can buy in tubs. Great for vegetarians.

Little Gnocchi with Truffle Oil, Butter and Sage

Topolini al Tartufo e Salvia SERVES 2

300g floury potatoes (such as King Edward), unpeeled

1 small egg, lightly beaten

100g plain flour, plus extra for dusting

100g salted butter

120g mixed wild mushrooms

1 tablespoon finely sliced fresh sage leaves

2 tablespoons truffle-flavoured olive oil

30g freshly grated Parmesan cheese

Salt and freshly ground black pepper

Put the potatoes into a large saucepan, cover with cold water and bring to the boil. Cook for 25–30 minutes until tender. Drain well and leave to cool slightly.

Peel the potatoes and press through a potato ricer into a large bowl. While the potatoes are still warm, add 2 pinches of salt, the egg and the flour. Lightly mix then turn out onto a floured surface. Knead lightly until you have soft, slightly sticky dough. (Do not overwork it or the little gnocchi will be tough.)

Cut the dough in half and roll each piece into a long sausage shape, about 1.5cm in diameter. Slice into 2cm pieces.

Lay the topolini on a lightly floured clean tea-towel.

Bring a large saucepan of salted water to the boil. Drop in the topolini, a few at a time, and cook for about 2 minutes. They are ready as soon as they float to the surface.

Meanwhile, melt the butter in a large frying pan over a medium heat. Once hot, stir in the mushrooms and cook for 2 minutes before adding the sage. Season with salt and pepper and remove the pan from the heat.

Add the topolini to the frying pan and toss well.

Divide between two serving plates, drizzle with the truffle oil and serve sprinkled with the Parmesan. Great with a glass of Prosecco.

Spicy Carrot Soup with Garlic Croûtons

Zuppa di Carote Piccante con Crostini all'Aglio SERVES 2

4 tablespoons olive oil

½ onion, chopped

250g carrots, peeled and cut into 1cm cubes

1 teaspoon chilli powder

350ml vegetable stock

2 garlic cloves, crushed

2 slices of white bread, crusts removed and cut into 1cm cubes

Salt

Heat half the oil in a saucepan and gently fry the onion for 3 minutes, stirring occasionally. Add the carrots with the chilli powder and continue to cook for a further 5 minutes, stirring occasionally.

Pour in the stock, bring to the boil and gently cook, with the lid on, for about 45 minutes.

Meanwhile, heat the remaining oil in a frying pan, add the garlic and fry on a low heat for 30 seconds. Add the bread cubes, turn the heat to medium and toss together for a few minutes until golden brown all over. Toss frequently. Drain on kitchen paper and keep warm.

Purée the soup in a food processor until smooth and season with salt. Return the soup to the rinsed-out saucepan and reheat gently.

Serve hot, sprinkled with the garlic croûtons.

Fresh and Tasty Tomato Salad

Insalata di Pomodori e Origano SERVES 2

4 large, beautifully ripe, plum tomatoes

4 tablespoons good-quality extra virgin olive oil

1 teaspoon dried oregano

Maldon sea salt and freshly ground black pepper

Use a sharp knife to slice the tomatoes into ½cm rounds and arrange on a serving plate. Drizzle over the oil, season with salt and pepper, and sprinkle with the oregano.

Leave to marinate, at room temperature, for at least 20 minutes before dishing up. Serve with crusty bread to mop up all the juice.

I know many people who don't really like the taste of shellfish, but are always very impressed with this recipe because, with the black pepper coating, the scallops become less fishy than usual. The fresh Italian salsa is a combination that you will never forget and is a perfect main course for a romantic dinner. To get the best flavour, make sure you use good pitted black olives and do not overcook the scallops otherwise they will lose their tenderness.

Scallops Coated in Black Pepper with Salsa

Capesante al Pepe con Salsetta SERVES 2

FOR THE SALSA

2 tablespoons olive oil

1 garlic clove, finely sliced

2 large plum tomatoes, chopped, seeds and skin included

30g black olives, pitted and cut in half

1 tablespoon salted capers, rinsed

5 basil leaves, sliced

Salt

FOR THE SCALLOPS

6 tablespoons fine breadcrumbs, toasted

50g plain flour

3 tablespoons black peppercorns, crushed

2 medium eggs, beaten and seasoned

8 scallops (ask your fishmonger to clean them)

4 tablespoons olive oil

30g salted butter

Extra virgin olive oil for drizzling

To make the salsa, heat the olive oil in a medium frying pan and fry the garlic over a medium heat until golden. Add the tomatoes, olives and capers, season with salt and cook for about 3 minutes. Stir in the basil and remove the salsa from the heat. Set aside to cool.

Meanwhile, mix the breadcrumbs, flour and black pepper together on a plate and have the eggs ready in a bowl.

Wash the scallops under cold running water and pat dry on kitchen paper. Dip each one first into the egg, then coat in the breadcrumb mixture.

Heat the oil with the butter in a large frying pan and fry the scallops over a high heat for about 1 minute on each side. Once they look brown and crunchy, transfer to kitchen paper to drain any excess oil.

To serve, place the salsa in the centre of two serving plates and arrange 4 crispy scallops on top. Drizzle with extra virgin olive oil and accompany with warm crusty bread.

I absolutely love tempura recipes and I think that oysters made tempura style are amazing. Of course let's not forget that this dish will be a great romantic starter because oysters are an aphrodisiac. You can prepare the batter a good hour ahead, but please cook your oysters just before serving.

Oysters in Sesame Seeds and Black Pepper Tempura

Ostriche Fritte con Salsetta al Soya SERVES 2

10 Pacific oysters

1 litre sunflower oil for deep frying

30g plain flour

30g cornflour

1 tablespoon crushed black peppercorns

2 tablespoons sesame seeds

About 150ml ice-cold soda water (from a new bottle)

1 lemon, cut into 6 wedges

Salt

FOR THE DIPPING SAUCE

3 tablespoons dark soy sauce

3 tablespoons cold water

Juice of 2 lemon wedges (see above)

To open the oysters, cover your hand with a tea-towel, hold the shell and insert the tip of a sharp knife into the muscle between the two halves. Remove the oyster and place on kitchen paper to dry. (Keep the deeper shells for serving.)

Make the dipping sauce by mixing the soy sauce, water and the juice from 2 of the lemon wedges in a small bowl and divide between 2 dipping saucers.

Heat the oil in a medium, heavy-based saucepan to about 190°C (if you don't have a cooking thermometer, the oil is hot enough when a piece of bread dropped into the oil turns brown in 30 seconds).

Meanwhile, sift the flour and cornflour into a large bowl with a pinch of salt. Mix in the black pepper with the sesame seeds and start to pour in the cold soda water. Stir everything together until just mixed and still a little lumpy. (Ensure that the batter is very thin – it should be almost transparent around the oysters.)

Dip the oysters, one at a time, into the batter and fry in the hot oil for no longer than 1 minute. Drain on kitchen paper and place in the reserved shells.

Serve immediately with the dipping sauce and remaining lemon wedges, accompanied by your favourite green salad.

If you think that any romantic dish should involve using your fingers, this is definitely the ultimate finger-licking recipe. The only thing you will have to be careful about is to cook this on the day you buy the shellfish so that they are really fresh – and never on a Monday because it won't be fresh from the market. You can use fresh tomatoes instead of tinned and, of course, you can substitute fresh chilli with dried chilli.

Quick Stew of Mussels and Clams

Impepata di Cozze e Arselle SERVES 2

2 tablespoons extra virgin olive oil, plus extra for brushing

3 garlic cloves (2 finely sliced, 1 left whole)

¼ teaspoon crushed dried chillies

400g tinned chopped tomatoes

125ml cold water

300g mussels, cleaned (discard broken ones and any that do not close when tapped firmly)

300g clams, cleaned (discard broken ones and any that do not close when tapped firmly)

30ml dry white wine

2 tablespoons chopped fresh flat-leaf parsley

2 slices white rustic bread (preferably ciabatta)

Salt to taste

Heat the oil in a large saucepan over a medium heat and fry the sliced garlic and chillies for about 20 seconds. Add in the chopped tomatoes with the water and leave to simmer, uncovered, for 8 minutes.

Meanwhile, place the mussels and clams in a second large saucepan on the heat and pour in the wine. Cover with a lid and cook for 5 minutes until the shellfish have opened.

Once ready, transfer the shellfish into the pan with the tomato sauce. Include the cooking juices but do not pour in the last few spoonfuls of the juices in case there is any grit. Stir well together, add the parsley and leave to rest for 1 minute.

Brush the sliced bread with a little olive oil, place on a hot griddle pan and toast on both sides until crispy and smoky. Once ready, rub the slices with the whole clove of garlic and place in two soup bowls. Spoon the shellfish and sauce on top of the bread and serve immediately with your favourite glass of cold white wine.

I know that many people worry about cooking a dish that involves any kind of pastry, but please trust me when I say that this is the easiest recipe to prepare and your partner or friend will not be disappointed with the presentation and, of course, the flavour. The biggest tips I can give you are to make sure that your salmon is very fresh and that your oven has been preheated.

Salmon and Creamy Leek Parcels

Fagottini di Salmone e Porri SERVES 2

2 leeks, trimmed and chopped

2 knobs of salted butter, plus extra for brushing

100g mascarpone cheese

6 sheets of filo pastry (20 x 20cm)

30g unsalted butter, melted

2 skinless salmon fillets, about 100g each

Salt and freshly ground black pepper

Cook the leeks in a large frying pan with 3 tablespoons of water and the knobs of butter for about 10 minutes. Season with salt and pepper and stir occasionally. Transfer from the pan to a bowl and leave to cool.

Preheat the oven to 200°C/400°F/gas mark 6.

Once the leeks have cooled, mix in the mascarpone cheese.

To assemble the parcels, brush a sheet of filo with melted butter, than lay 2 more sheets on top, brushing with butter between each layer. Place a salmon fillet in the centre, season with salt and pepper then spoon half the leek mixture on top of each fillet. Fold the pastry ends over the top, pull up the sides and scrunch together to enclose the filling. Brush both parcels with melted butter.

Place the parcels on a lightly greased baking sheet and cook in the middle of the oven for 20 minutes until browned and crisp.

Serve with your favourite green salad.

It is very traditional, especially in northern Italy, around Pisa, to cook asparagus in puff pastry. I learnt this recipe about twenty years ago when, for the first time, I went to visit the famous tower of Pisa. It was a family friend who prepared it for us and I remember he told me that he won his wife with this dish. How romantic! Only use fresh asparagus for this dish and you can substitute the Parmesan cheese with Pecorino if you prefer.

Asparagus and Ricotta Tarts

Tartine di Asparagi e Ricotta SERVES 2

200g ready-rolled puff pastry, at room temperature

150g ricotta cheese

25g freshly grated Parmesan cheese

6 sun-dried tomatoes in oil, drained and finely chopped

10 asparagus spears

2 tablespoons extra virgin olive oil

1 tablespoon freshly chopped chives

Salt and freshly ground black pepper

Preheat the oven to 200°C/400°F/gas mark 6.

Unroll the pastry and cut into two rectangles, each about 16 x 12cm. Use a knife to mark out a smaller rectangle on each piece, big enough to hold 5 asparagus spears. (Do not cut through the pastry.) Use a small sharp knife to mark the borders in a neat lattice pattern. Transfer to a baking sheet.

Bake the pastry in the middle of the oven for about 15 minutes until just puffy and slightly coloured. Remove, set aside to cool slightly then gently depress the risen 'window' with the back of a fork.

Lightly mix together the ricotta with the Parmesan. Gently fold in the sun-dried tomatoes and season with salt and pepper.

Trim the asparagus spears to fit the pastry 'window'. Divide the ricotta mixture between the two pastry cases. Place the asparagus spears on top and slightly press into the ricotta mix.

Drizzle with the extra virgin olive oil and bake for 20 minutes.

Sprinkle the tarts with the chives and serve hot or at room temperature accompanied with a crispy salad.

SERVES
2

Honey Chicken Liver Salad with Sherry Vinegar

Insalata di Fegatielli e Pinoli SERVES 2

2 tablespoons olive oil

300g chicken livers

50g pine kernels

100g rocket leaves

1 tablespoon sherry vinegar

1 tablespoon runny honey

Salt and freshly ground black pepper

Heat the olive oil in a large frying pan and start to cook the livers with the pine kernels over a medium heat for about 6 minutes. Season with salt and pepper and stir occasionally to help the liver cook evenly.

Meanwhile, divide the rocket leaves between two serving plates.

Once the chicken livers are cooked, turn off the heat and pour in the sherry vinegar with the honey. Use a wooden spoon to deglaze the pan by stirring everything about and scraping the bottom of the pan.

Serve the livers on top of the rocket leaves and pour over the juices from the pan.

Perfetto with a big glass of red wine.

Honey-glazed Carrots with Macadamia Nuts

Carote Smielate SERVES 2

2 large carrots, peeled and cut into 1cm rounds

150g shallots, peeled

1 tablespoon salted butter

10 macadamia nuts, halved

1 tablespoon runny honey

Salt and freshly ground black pepper

Bring a medium saucepan of salted water to the boil and cook the carrots and shallots for 3 minutes. Drain.

Melt the butter in a large frying pan and add the shallots, carrots and nuts. Season with salt and pepper and fry over a medium heat for 5 minutes, stirring occasionally.

Pour in the honey and continue to cook, over a higher heat, for a further 2 minutes.

Serve hot with your favourite main course or allow to cool to room temperature and mix with salad leaves.

If you need a tasty and impressive recipe with not a lot of washing up to do, this is the one to try. Fish always goes down well for a fabulous romantic dinner because it's light, tasty and it cooks quickly. If you don't want to use turbot, try monkfish and make sure you have a good bottle of cold Italian wine to accompany it.

Roasted Turbot with Baby Leeks and Cherry Tomatoes

Rombo e Porri al Forno con Pomodorini SERVES 2

8 baby leeks, trimmed and washed

2 x 200g turbot fillets (off the bone), scaled and skin on

2 tablespoons fresh rosemary leaves, stripped from the stalks

2 tablespoons fresh thyme leaves

3 tablespoons extra virgin olive oil

1 small lemon, quartered

10 cherry tomatoes

Salt and freshly ground black pepper

Bring a saucepan of salted water to the boil and cook the leeks for about 3 minutes. Drain in a colander and allow to steam dry.

Place the fish in a large bowl with the herbs, olive oil, lemon quarters and season with salt and pepper. Add in the leeks, toss well and leave to rest for 15 minutes.

Meanwhile, preheat the oven to 200°C/400°F/gas mark 6. Put in a roasting tin to warm up.

Place the fish, skin-side down, on the preheated roasting tin and pour over the rest of the ingredients from the bowl. Roast for 15 minutes, then remove the fish and keep warm.

Add the cherry tomatoes to the roasting tin and continue to roast the leeks for a further 5 minutes.

Remove the tin from the oven and pile the leeks onto two warm serving plates. Place the fish on top and drizzle with the cooking juices.

Arrange the cherry tomatoes around the plates. Serve immediately with a cold glass of Pinot Grigio.

This recipe is for Nicole, who gave me the inspiration for it. Scallops are one of the most romantic ingredients you can cook – luxurious, soft and succulent. They have a very delicate taste so you don't want too many strong flavours with them, but the salty pancetta will go with it perfectly. You can leave the roe in if you don't want to waste anything.

Creamy Scallops with Pancetta

Capesante alla Nicoletta SERVES 2

50g butter

1 onion, diced

50ml double cream

Vegetable oil for frying

1 large leek, trimmed and cut into thin matchsticks

100g diced pancetta

6 large scallops, cleaned, roe removed

Salt and freshly ground black pepper

Melt half the butter in a frying pan. When it foams, add the onion and cook over a low heat for 15 minutes until the onion is soft but not coloured. Stir in the cream and cook for 2 more minutes. Blend to a smooth purée and keep warm.

Heat the vegetable oil in another frying pan and shallow-fry the leek until slightly coloured and crispy. Remove from the pan and drain on kitchen paper. Fry off the pancetta for 2–3 minutes or until it begins to crisp up. Remove from the pan and pour out any excess fat.

Season the scallops. Return the frying pan to the heat, add the remaining butter to the hot pan along with the scallops. Fry the scallops for 10–15 seconds on one side or until they start to caramelise. Flip the scallops, add the pancetta and remove from the heat.

Place 2 tablespoons of the onion purée in the centre of each warmed plate. Arrange 3 scallops on the purée and spoon over the pancetta along with some of the buttery juices. Top with a small handful of the crispy leeks.

Serve immediately with a cold glass of Champagne!!

This is one of my mother's special Sunday recipes. I remember when I was a child, my father going to the fish market to buy the fresh prawns, bringing them home and waiting impatiently for my mum to cook them in this delicious sauce. This is what I call a romantic dish.

King Prawns in Caper and Tomato Sauce

Gamberoni alla Marinara SERVES 2

3 tablespoons olive oil

3 tinned anchovy fillets in oil, drained

1 garlic clove, finely sliced

2 tablespoons pitted Kalamata black olives

1 tablespoon salted capers, rinsed and drained

400g tinned chopped tomatoes

1 teaspoon dried oregano

8 large king prawns (head and shells on)

Salt and freshly ground black pepper

Heat the oil in a large frying pan and cook the anchovies until they dissolve. Add the garlic and continue to fry until soft and golden. Stir in the olives and capers. Pour in the chopped tomatoes with the oregano, season with salt and pepper and simmer, uncovered, for about 15 minutes. Stir occasionally.

Add the prawns to the sauce and continue to cook gently for 4 minutes. Turn the prawns over and cook for another 4 minutes.

Place some of the sauce in the middle of two serving plates and top with 4 prawns. Try to cross 2 prawns together so that they sit up on the plate.

Accompany the dish with your favourite salad and some warm crusty bread, and enjoy with a glass of cold Prosecco.

The first time I cooked this recipe was about five years ago and even today I still believe that this is my lucky dish. It was the recipe that I cooked on my first ever television show with Jenni Barnett and is still a big hit with the ladies. I know that you may ask how a plate of pasta can be a big hit with the ladies and my answer is very simple, trust me – I'm Italian! You can substitute pork mince with beef or lamb mince and you can stuff the pasta a good couple of hours in advance.

Stuffed Pasta Shells

Conchiglioni Ripieni SERVES 2

150g dry conchiglioni (10 shells)

½ onion, finely chopped

3 tablespoons olive oil

250g minced pork (or beef or lamb, if you prefer)

250g béchamel sauce (you can use ready-made)

400g tinned chopped tomatoes

8 basil leaves

50g freshly grated Parmesan cheese

Salt and freshly ground black pepper

Parboil the pasta in boiling salted water for about 5 minutes. Drain, place on a clean tea-towel and leave to cool.

Fry the onion in a large frying pan in 2 tablespoons of the olive oil until golden brown. Add the mince and mix well allowing the meat to crumble. Cook, stirring frequently, for 15 minutes until the meat has browned. Remove from the heat and leave to cool.

Once the mince has cooled down, pour half of the cold béchamel sauce into the pan and mix with the mince.

Tip the tomatoes into a small saucepan and heat through. When bubbling, add the remaining olive oil, the basil and season with salt and pepper. Cook for no longer than 3 minutes.

Preheat the oven to 180°C/350°F/gas mark 4.

Pour the tomato sauce into the bottom of an ovenproof dish (this prevents the pasta shells from sticking).

Use a tablespoon to fill the conchiglioni with the meat mixture and gently place them in the dish. Make sure the shells aren't too close together. When you have filled the dish, drizzle the pasta with the remaining béchamel, and cover the dish with foil.

Bake for about 20 minutes. Remove the foil, sprinkle with the Parmesan and cook for a further 5–10 minutes or until the cheese is golden.

Serve immediately by spooning some of the tomato sauce into the centre of a serving plate and arranging the pasta shells on top.

What can I say about this recipe? Everyone has tried it, most people love it, but not many people know how to cook it properly. If you read the ingredients. you have probably realised that there is no cream in this recipe – that's how you cook a traditional spaghetti carbonara. For romantic effect, serve all the pasta in a large bowl, sit close and share.

Pasta with Smoked Pancetta, Eggs and Pecorino Romano

Spaghetti alla Carbonara SERVES 2

1 tablespoon extra virgin olive oil

50g salted butter

100g smoked pancetta, rind removed, cut into small pieces

250g dry spaghetti

3 large egg yolks, beaten

2 tablespoons finely chopped fresh flat-leaf parsley

30g freshly grated Pecorino Romano cheese

Salt and freshly ground black pepper

Heat the oil and the butter together in a large frying pan over a medium heat. Add the pancetta with a pinch of black pepper and fry until very crispy, stirring occasionally.

Meanwhile, cook the pasta in a large saucepan with plenty of boiling salted water (for up to 300g pasta allow at least 4 litres water) until al dente. Once the pasta is cooked, drain thoroughly and place in the hot frying pan with the pancetta.

Remove the pan from the heat, then pour in the eggs with the parsley. Stirring continuously add 4–5 tablespoons hot water until you create a creamy texture. Season lightly with salt (go easy because the pancetta can be quite salty). Serve immediately topped with the grated cheese.

There are two things that my wife can't get enough of. First, well I leave it to your imagination. Second is this dish. Traditionally this recipe is cooked with white wine, but one day I didn't have any and the only bottle I had in the fridge was sweet Martini Bianco – what a wonderful experiment. Try veal instead of chicken and if you don't have sweet vermouth, you can use a good Marsala wine. Make sure that the chicken is thin, so it cooks fast and doesn't get tough.

Breast of Chicken in Martini Sauce

Scaloppine di Pollo al Martini SERVES 2

2 medium skinless chicken breasts

4 tablespoons plain flour

60g salted butter, plus a little extra for the sauce

150ml Martini Bianco (sweet)

Salt and freshly ground black pepper

Place the chicken breasts on a chopping board, cut in half horizontally and lay a piece of clingfilm on top. Use a meat mallet to flatten the breasts to a thickness of 5mm.

Put the flour on a flat plate and season with salt and pepper.

Melt the butter in a large frying pan over a medium heat.

Lay the chicken breasts in the seasoned flour and lightly coat on both sides. Place in the pan and gently fry in the butter for about 3 minutes on one side. Turn over and cook for a further minute.

Pour in the Martini and using a match or lighter, flame the alcohol. Allow the alcohol to burn off, then cook for a further 2 minutes and season with salt.

Place the scaloppine on a serving plate.

Add an extra knob of butter to the pan. Mix well over a medium heat then pour immediately over the chicken.

I like to serve this with a simple salad of spinach leaves dressed with extra virgin olive oil, a squeeze of fresh lemon juice and a pinch of sea salt.

Whenever I need to be forgiven by my wife, I know that there are only two things that can save me — an expensive present or my fillet steak with flamed brandy. She absolutely adores it and I also think she likes to see a man flaming in her kitchen. Well I'm going to dedicate this recipe to all the men out there that need to be forgiven and hope it works for you. Please, please do not overcook the steak otherwise the recipe will be completely ruined.

Fillet Steak with Flamed Brandy and Green Peppercorns

Filetto al Pepe Verde e Brandy con Patate al Forno SERVES 2

FOR THE OVEN CHIPS

2 baking potatoes, scrubbed and cut into chunky chips

2 sprigs of fresh rosemary

3 garlic cloves, unpeeled and slightly crushed

2 tablespoons olive oil

Salt and freshly ground black pepper

FOR THE STEAK

2 teaspoons coarsely ground black pepper

2 fillet steaks, about 150g each

1 tablespoon olive oil

2 knobs of butter

2 tablespoons brandy

2 tablespoons dry white wine

50ml beef stock

1 tablespoon green peppercorns in brine, drained

70ml double cream

Preheat the oven to 220°C/450°F/gas mark 8.

Place the potatoes, rosemary and garlic on a large non-stick baking tray. Drizzle over the olive oil, season with salt and pepper and cook in the middle of the oven for 30 minutes until the chips are cooked through and crisp. Check and turn them occasionally.

Meanwhile, rub the coarsely ground black pepper all over the steaks.

Heat the oil with 1 knob of butter in a medium frying pan. As soon as the butter stops foaming, add the steaks. Cook for 4 minutes on each side for a medium steak, or for 3 minutes if you like it rare. Transfer the steaks to a warm plate, season with salt and set aside in a warm place to rest for 3 minutes.

Pour the excess fat from the pan then add the brandy. Using a match or lighter, flame the alcohol. Allow the alcohol to burn off, then stir the pan, scraping the meat juices off the bottom of the pan. Pour in the white wine and reduce by half.

Add the stock and continue to cook over a high heat, stirring occasionally, until the sauce is well reduced.

Stir in the peppercorns, the cream and the remaining butter. Cook for a further 2 minutes stirring continuously.

Pile the chips in the middle of two serving plates and top each one with the fillet steak. Pour over the sauce and serve immediately with a glass of dry red wine.

Come on, this is the romantic chapter so of course I had to put in a banana recipe and I couldn't think of anything better than crispy chunks of banana served with a delicious caramel sauce. Unfortunately you will not be able to cook the bananas ahead so you need to prepare them at the last minute but they do say, good things come to those who wait and whoever is waiting for this won't be disappointed. If you fancy, you can use apples instead.

Banana Fritters with Quick Caramel Sauce

Frittelle di Banana SERVES 2

FOR THE CARAMEL SAUCE

90g salted butter

200g soft brown sugar

120ml double cream

FOR THE FRITTERS

125g self-raising flour

1 egg, beaten

190ml cold soda water (don't open the bottle until the last minute)

2 bananas, cut into 3cm chunks

Oil for deep frying

Icing sugar for dusting

To make the sauce, place the butter, sugar and cream in a small saucepan. Bring to the boil, reduce the heat and simmer for 3 minutes. Set aside.

Sift the flour into a bowl, make a well in the centre and add the egg and the soda all at once. Stir until all the liquid is incorporated and the batter is free of lumps.

Heat the oil in a deep heavy-based pan. When a cube of bread browns in 15 seconds it is hot enough.

Dip the bananas in the batter a few pieces at a time, drain off any excess and gently lower the pieces into the hot oil using a slotted spoon. Cook for about 2 minutes or until golden, crisp and warmed through.

Carefully remove the fritters from the oil with the slotted spoon and drain on kitchen paper. Repeat with the remaining banana pieces.

Serve the fritters immediately with the caramel sauce and dusted all over with plenty of icing sugar. Fantastic with a little glass of Vin Santo or any other dessert wine.

I can still see myself as a teenager sitting outside a bar in my home town of Torre del Greco, having this exquisite dessert with all my friends from school. This is the one to choose if you want to impress someone with something easy to make. Make sure you use a good-quality vanilla ice cream and if you don't like Amaretto liqueur, try Baileys instead.

Vanilla Ice Cream with Hot Espresso, Amaretto and Grated Chocolate

Affogato al Caffe e Amaretto SERVES 2

250g tub good-quality vanilla ice cream

2 shots freshly made espresso

2 tablespoons Amaretto liqueur

2 teaspoons grated good-quality dark chocolate

Drop 2 scoops of ice cream into two stemmed glasses or cappuccino cups. Pour over the freshly made hot coffee and 1 tablespoon of the Amaretto liqueur per serving.

Sprinkle the affogato with grated chocolate and serve immediately with chocolate cantuccini or your favourite Italian biscuits.

PS Affogato has to be made with proper strong espresso coffee, so unless you have the right machine, save the pleasure for the next time you are at my house or in an Italian restaurant.

I must have been about sixteen, and I can remember it like it was yesterday – my first exam at my catering college. The night before I could not sleep thinking about what I was going to prepare for my exam and, knowing that the judge was a lady, I thought a hot chocolate fondant should do the job. Well... I was right – I came first in the class and got about six dates with girls who wanted to try it!

Hot Chocolate Fondants Stuffed with Chocolate Truffles

Paradiso di Cioccolato SERVES 2

100g good-quality dark chocolate
(70 per cent cocoa solids)

50g salted butter, at room temperature

20g ground almonds

20g cornflour

1 eggs, separated

45g caster sugar

1 tablespoons Amaretto liqueur

3 good-quality chocolate truffles

Icing sugar, for dusting

Preheat the oven to 160°C/325°F/gas mark 3.

Finely grate about 25g of the chocolate onto a plate.

Rub 25g of the butter all over the inside of 2 tall dariole moulds, dust well with the grated chocolate, shake any excess and set aside on a baking tray.

Melt the remaining chocolate plus any leftover grated chocolate and the remaining butter in a large heatproof bowl set over a pan of simmering water.

Remove the bowl from the heat and beat the ground almonds, cornflour and egg yolks into the melted chocolate.

In a separate, large, clean, dry bowl, whisk the egg white until soft peaks forms. Gradually whisk in the caster sugar.

Fold the meringue mixture and the Amaretto liqueur into the melted chocolate mixture.

Gently spoon half of the mixture into the moulds, place a chocolate truffle on top then continue to fill the moulds leaving a gap of about 5mm at the top.

Bake the fondants in the middle of the oven for 20 minutes until risen and slightly wobbly.

Turn the fondants out onto 2 serving plates, dust liberally with icing sugar and serve them hot.

Per Me

Recipes for one

Coming home from the studios one evening

after recording *Ready Steady Cook*, a taxi driver recognised me and we started talking about food. One of the things he said really frustrated him was that no one seemed to write books for people that live on their own or for that one night when you only need to cook for one. He explained that following a recipe that was created for four but using smaller amounts of ingredients never seemed to work. I couldn't agree more with him so here they are... recipes for the nights you are alone but still want to cook something nice. I have also created recipes that you can make in big batches and freeze very easily so you can defrost and heat up anytime you want during the week. So for those who live on their own – there is no longer any excuse not to get in the kitchen and start cooking.

After a great boys' night out, this is probably the best dish to have, either when you come back or when you finally get up in the morning. Of course it reminds me of my playboy days, long, long ago. The unique combination of Brie with the crispy pancetta is absolutely *Buonissimo*, though you can definitely substitute the pancetta with streaky bacon or the Brie with a strong Cheddar cheese. Try to serve my eggs as shown on the photograph.

Playboy Eggs

Uova alla Playboy SERVES 1

4 slices pancetta,
2 chopped into small
pieces

1 tablespoon olive
oil, plus extra for
greasing

50g button
mushrooms,
quartered

1 spring onion,
sliced on the
diagonal

30g ripe Brie cheese,
cut into small
chunks

2 fresh eggs

Salt and freshly
ground black pepper

Preheat the oven to 200°C/400°F/gas mark 6 and grease a cappuccino cup with a little olive oil.

Place the two whole slices of pancetta on a baking tray and cook in the oven until golden and crispy. Leave to cool until firm.

Heat the olive oil in a medium frying pan and fry the mushrooms and the chopped pancetta for about 5 minutes until golden. Add the spring onion, season and cook for a further 3 minutes, stirring continuously. Remove from the heat and stir in half the cheese.

Pour the mixture into the greased cup then break the eggs in the cup, keeping the yolks whole. Place on a baking tray and bake, uncovered, for 5 minutes.

Remove from the oven, sprinkle the remaining cheese over the eggs and bake, uncovered, for a further 8 minutes.

Once ready, stand the slices of crispy pancetta either side of the cup so that they look like the ears of the playboy bunny. Sprinkle with black pepper.

Serve immediately with your favourite bread.

Apart from quickly boiling the beans, there is not really a lot of cooking for this recipe so you have no excuses for not getting these few ingredients together and making this wonderful salad. I often assemble this dish when I can't really be bothered to cook and I'm in need of something fresh, colourful and tasty. If you prefer, you can substitute the goat's cheese with chunks of mozzarella and you can also add any nuts that you fancy.

French Bean Salad with Mint, Goat's Cheese and Pine Kernels

Fagiolini alla Menta con Formaggio di Capra e Pinoli SERVES 1

100g French beans, trimmed

½ garlic clove

3 fresh mint leaves

2 tablespoons extra virgin olive oil

1 tablespoon freshly squeezed lemon juice

70g firm goat's cheese

2 tablespoons pine kernels, toasted in a dry frying pan

Salt and freshly ground black pepper

Cook the beans in boiling salted water until al dente.

Meanwhile, finely chop the garlic and the mint together and place in a large bowl. Pour in the oil and lemon juice and mix together until well combined.

Drain the beans well and add to the bowl with the dressing. Season with salt and pepper and toss everything together until evenly coated.

Transfer the salad to a serving plate, crumble over the goat's cheese and scatter with the cooled pine kernels. Enjoy with some warm crusty bread.

Herby Potato Cakes with Bubbling Goat's Cheese

Crocchette di Patate e Formaggio di Capra SERVES 1

200g floury potatoes (such as King Edward, peeled)

2 teaspoons chopped fresh thyme leaves, plus 1–2 sprigs for garnish

1 spring onion, finely chopped

2 tablespoons olive oil

1 knob of salted butter

60g firm goat's cheese

Salt and freshly ground black pepper

Coarsely grate the potatoes, then use your hands to squeeze out as much of the thick starchy liquid as possible. Place into a large bowl and combine with the thyme and chopped spring onion. Season with salt and pepper.

Divide the mixture into two and shape into two flattish discs about 1.5cm thick.

Heat the oil and the butter in a frying pan. Lower the potato cakes into the pan, spacing them well apart and cook over a medium heat. Press firmly down with a spatula and cook for 4 minutes on each side until golden.

Preheat the grill to a medium heat.

Once the cakes are ready, cut the cheese in half horizontally and place one half, cut side up, on each potato cake. Grill for about 3 minutes until lightly golden.

Transfer immediately to a serving plate, garnish with thyme sprigs and accompany with some rocket leaves.

Warm Potato and Crispy Bacon Salad

Patate e Pancetta MAKES 4 PORTIONS, BUT WILL KEEP WELL IN THE FRIDGE FOR A FEW DAYS

900g baby new potatoes, scrubbed

1 tablespoon olive oil

5 rashers bacon

½ tablespoon wholegrain mustard

1 tablespoon white wine vinegar

1 spring onion, finely sliced

4 tablespoons pumpkin seeds

Salt and freshly ground black pepper

Bring a large saucepan of salted water to the boil and cook the potatoes for about 18 minutes or until tender. Drain and cut in half.

Meanwhile, heat the oil in a frying pan and cook the bacon until very crispy. Transfer to a plate and allow to cool. Cut into small pieces.

Place the warm potatoes in a large bowl and pour in the mustard and the vinegar. Add in the spring onion and half the bacon. Season with salt and pepper and toss everything together.

When you are ready to serve, transfer the salad to a large serving dish. Sprinkle with the pumpkin seeds and the remaining crispy bacon.

When I first came to London, I could not understand why anyone would mix a boiled prawn with mayonnaise and the other ingredients that go into a prawn cocktail sauce. Now I am completely converted, but of course I could not stick to the original recipe – I had to put my Italian twist to this classic British dish. Make sure you use big juicy prawns and good-quality green pitted olives.

Italian Prawn Cocktail

SERVES 1

1 tablespoon mayonnaise

1 tablespoon double cream

½ teaspoon tomato purée

1 teaspoon freshly squeezed lemon juice

Dash of Worcestershire sauce

1 teaspoon small capers in brine, drained

1 tablespoon green pitted olives, chopped

8 cooked, peeled prawns

Handful of lettuce leaves, shredded

Slices of lemon, to garnish

Salt and freshly ground black pepper

Put the mayonnaise into a bowl and mix in the cream, tomato purée, lemon juice, Worcestershire sauce, capers, and olives.

Fold in the prawns and season with salt and pepper.

At the last minute, fold in the lettuce and transfer immediately to a large Martini glass garnished with lemon slices.

Buonissimo with slices of toasted brown bread.

The worst thing you can do to asparagus is to overcook it, unless of course, you're making this wonderful soup. Never, ever try to create this dish with tinned asparagus because you will completely lose the freshness of the dish. I chose this soup for this chapter, first of all because of the taste, and secondly because, if there is any left over, you can freeze it as long as you use it up within ten days.

Spring Chilled Asparagus Soup

Zuppa di Asparagi SERVES 1, FREEZE THE REMAINING SOUP

400g asparagus

2 tablespoons salted butter

2 onions, chopped

1 litre vegetable stock

100ml single cream

Zest of 1 unwaxed lemon, to garnish

Salt and white pepper

Cut the tips from the asparagus stalks, about 5cm from the top. Drop into a medium saucepan of boiling salted water and cook for 3 minutes. Drain and immediately refresh in cold water. Set aside.

With the help of a potato peeler, scrape the asparagus stalks and discard the woody ends. Chop the remaining stalks.

Melt the butter in a large saucepan and cook the onions with the chopped stalks over a medium heat for 10 minutes. Stir occasionally.

Pour in the stock and season with salt and pepper. Bring to the boil and simmer over a medium heat for 35 minutes until everything is tender. Once cooked, allow to cool.

Pour the soup into a blender or food processor and blitz until smooth. Pass through a sieve into a bowl and then stir in the cream.

Cover the bowl with clingfilm and refrigerate for 2 hours.

Garnish with the reserved asparagus tips and a few strands of lemon zest and serve. Any remaining soup can be frozen.

I love liver, but the problem I have with it is that most of the time people try to do too much with it, or even worse they overcook it. This is a very traditional Italian way to cook liver and, in my family, it is the only way we cook it. Please, please, please do not use dried sage because you will completely ruin this dish.

Calfs' Liver with Black Pepper, Butter and Sage

Fegato al Burro, Salvia e Pepe SERVES 1

8 cherry tomatoes on the vine

3 tablespoons olive oil

1 slice ciabatta

3 tablespoons plain flour, for dusting

100g calfs' liver

30g salted butter

4 fresh sage leaves

Handful of mixed salad leaves

Salt and freshly ground black pepper

Preheat the oven to 200°C/400°F/gas mark 6.

Place the cherry tomatoes on a small roasting tray, Drizzle with 1 tablespoon of the olive oil, season well and place in the oven for 5–10 minutes until soft and slightly roasted.

Next griddle or toast the ciabatta and set aside.

Place the flour on a plate and use to coat the liver on both sides.

Heat the remaining olive oil in a medium frying pan over a high heat. Once hot, cook the liver for 30 seconds on each side or, if you like your liver well done, cook for 50 seconds on each side.

Lower the heat to medium, wipe out any oil left in the frying pan and add the butter and the sage leaves. Season with salt and plenty of black pepper. Continue to cook for about 40 seconds, just until the butter is completely melted.

Dress the liver with the butter and sage sauce and serve immediately on top of the ciabatta, so that the bread can soak up the lovely buttery juices. Perfect with your favourite crispy salad and the roasted cherry tomatoes.

Fegato al Burro, Salvia e Pepe

SERVES
1

I think that as I get older I like curries more and more. I have to admit that I can only manage a medium-hot one, but slowly, slowly I'll get there. When I first came to England, I didn't really appreciate the fantastic flavours of spices and, now, fourteen years later, I've written this recipe which I've very proudly named Italian Bean Curry. You can use dried beans, but I think the tinned ones work perfectly for this kind of dish.

Italian Bean Curry

Fagioli al Curry SERVES 1, FREEZE THE REMAINING 3 PORTIONS

2 tablespoons olive oil

4 tablespoons good-quality curry paste

400ml coconut milk

100ml vegetable stock

200g (drained weight) tinned cannellini beans

200g (drained weight) tinned borlotti beans

100g (drained weight) tinned lentils

3 spring onions, finely sliced

2 large plum tomatoes, skinned and cut into 1cm cubes

Lime wedges, to garnish

Put the oil in a medium saucepan over a medium heat and add the curry paste. Cook for 3 minutes, stirring occasionally.

Pour in the coconut milk with the stock, bring to the boil and simmer, uncovered, for 5 minutes. Add in the beans, lentils, onions and tomatoes. Continue to simmer for a further 5 minutes, stirring occasionally.

Serve with plain rice of your choice, with a lime wedge on top.

Most of my food memories growing up in Italy consist of seafood. We ate it almost every day because we lived by the coast – I always remember this particular dish because I used to go fishing with my uncle (Mazza Tosta) who used to be (and I hope still is) the master of cooking razor clams. The combination of garlic, chilli, parsley and clams works beautifully especially if you serve it with a good country-style bread.

Razor Clams with Olive Oil, Lime and Chilli

Cannollicchi alla Zio Salvatore SERVES 1

2 slices country-style bread

3 tablespoons olive oil

Pinch of dried chilli flakes

8 razor clams, washed, but still in their shells

1 tablespoon finely chopped fresh flat-leaf parsley

1 garlic clove

Lime wedges, to garnish

Sea salt

First toast the bread on both sides in a toaster or under the grill. Leave to cool slightly.

Heat the oil with the chilli flakes in a large frying pan, and add the clams in a single layer, hinge side down.

Once the clams have completely opened, turn them over, ensuring that the meat comes into contact with the base of the pan. Sprinkle with the parsley and a little sea salt and cook for 1 minute until the clams are lightly browned.

Meanwhile, rub the garlic clove over one side of the toasted bread.

Serve the clams immediately with the garlic toasted bread, the fresh lime wedges and enjoy with a cold glass of Italian beer.

I have to admit that I don't often cook sea bream. I usually order it when I'm out in a restaurant especially when I'm in the south of Italy, but since I put this recipe together, I cook it at least twice a month. I love the way the rosemary and the garlic work with the fish and, even better, it cooks in only twenty minutes. You can change the sea bream for sea bass and make sure that you drizzle it with a good-quality extra virgin olive oil.

Roast Sea Bream with Rosemary and Garlic

Orata al Forno con Aglio e Rosmarino SERVES 1

1 whole sea bream (about 400g), scaled and gutted

5 sprigs fresh rosemary

2 garlic cloves, unpeeled and halved

2 tablespoons olive oil

40g rocket leaves

¼ fennel bulb, thinly sliced

¼ radicchio, roughly chopped

1 lemon, half for juicing, half for serving

1 tablespoon extra virgin olive oil

Maldon sea salt and freshly ground black pepper

Preheat the oven to 200°C/400°F/gas mark 6.

Place the fish on a chopping board and use a sharp knife to slash each side twice diagonally.

Insert 3 of the rosemary sprigs and all the garlic into the cavity and stick the remaining rosemary into the slashes. (Allow these seasonings to hang out of the fish so that they too will roast, giving extra flavour to the dish.)

Place the fish in a roasting tin, drizzle with the olive oil and sprinkle with sea salt. Roast in the oven for 20 minutes until the flesh is white and the skin crispy.

Meanwhile, dress the rocket leaves, fennel and radicchio in a bowl with the juice of half the lemon and the extra virgin olive oil. Season with salt and pepper and mix well.

Serve the fish hot from the oven accompanied with a beautiful fresh salad and the other half of the lemon.

I know that it may sound a bit cheesy to dedicate a recipe to yourself, but really guys, this is the kind of dish that I like to prepare when I'm on my own and I'm in need of something tasty and easy. Make sure you rest the steak for a good minute after it has been cooked allowing the meat to get tender, and dress and season the rocket leaves just before you are ready to eat.

Sliced Steak with Cherry Tomatoes, Rocket and Balsamic Vinegar Dressing

Tagliata alla Gino SERVES 1

1 sirloin steak
(about 250g)

3 tablespoons extra
virgin olive oil

5 cherry tomatoes,
washed and halved

50g rocket leaves

1 tablespoon good-
quality balsamic
vinegar

10 pieces freshly
shaved Parmesan
cheese

Salt and freshly
ground black pepper

Rub the steak with 1 tablespoon of the oil and make little cuts along the fat to stop the meat shrinking and curving as it cooks.

Preheat a griddle pan until hot and cook the steak for 2 minutes on each side for medium-cooked (add an extra 2 minutes on each side if you prefer your steak well done). Season with salt and pepper and place the steak on a chopping board to rest for 1 minute.

Meanwhile, place the tomatoes and rocket leaves in a large bowl, pour over the remaining oil, season, and mix well with your fingertips. Arrange the salad on a serving plate.

Use a sharp knife to cut the steak into 2cm slices and lay on the salad. Drizzle over the balsamic vinegar and scatter with the Parmesan.

Serve immediately with a cold beer.

Cavoletti Gratinati

I wanted to write this recipe mainly because I want people to know that Brussels sprouts are not just for Christmas. They can be used all year round and, combined with the right ingredients, are a delicious side dish to any main course especially a meat one. You can try this recipe with carrots or fresh fennel instead of Brussels sprouts.

Brussels Sprouts with Garlic Breadcrumbs and Pecorino

Cavoletti Gratinati SERVES 1

120g Brussels sprouts

3 tablespoons extra virgin olive oil, plus extra for drizzling

3 tablespoons dried breadcrumbs

3 tablespoons freshly grated Pecorino Romano cheese

2 tablespoons finely chopped fresh flat-leaf parsley

1 garlic clove, finely chopped

Salt and freshly ground black pepper

Preheat the oven to 220°C/425°F/gas mark 7.

Parboil the Brussels sprouts in boiling salted water for 5 minutes. Drain thoroughly.

Drizzle 2 tablespoons of the oil in an ovenproof oval dish just big enough to hold all the sprouts.

Mix together the breadcrumbs, the cheese, parsley, garlic and the remaining oil in a small bowl. Season with salt and pepper. Sprinkle the mixture over the Brussels sprouts.

Put the dish in the middle of the oven and cook for 15 minutes.

Remove from the oven, drizzle with a little more oil and serve as a main dish or to accompany a meat dish of your choice.

If you come in late from work and you are starving, this is a really quick and filling meal to prepare, yet doesn't sit heavily on your stomach because of the freshness of the lemon and the lightness of the courgettes. Make sure that once the pasta is combined into the sauce, you serve it immediately otherwise it will get claggy. I have also tried this recipe without the Parmesan cheese and it works fine. And, of course, make sure the spaghetti is al dente.

Courgettes and Lemon Zest Pasta

Spaghetti con Zucchine e Buccia di Limone SERVES 1

1 courgette, coarsely grated

3 tablespoons olive oil

Good pinch of dried chilli flakes

2 tablespoons pine kernels

Zest of ¼ unwaxed lemon

120g spaghetti

2 tablespoons freshly grated Parmesan cheese

Salt

Put the grated courgettes in a clean tea-towel and squeeze dry.

Heat the oil in a large frying pan and fry the courgette for 5 minutes over a medium heat, stirring occasionally. Add the chilli flakes, pine kernels and lemon zest and continue to cook for a further 3 minutes. Season with salt and stir.

Meanwhile, cook the pasta in a large saucepan with plenty of boiling salted water until al dente. Once the pasta is cooked, drain thoroughly and tip into the frying pan with the courgette.

Toss everything together over a medium heat for 30 seconds. Serve immediately, sprinkled with Parmesan.

If you fancy making yourself a really special meal, this is the one for you. The Parma ham will keep the chicken breast from drying out in the oven, and as you are by yourself, you won't have to worry about garlic breath! If you love this recipe, you can easily double or quadruple the quantities and make it for your friends and family.

Chicken Wrapped in Parma Ham with a Creamy Herb Sauce

Pollo Avvolto con Prosciutto Crudo SERVES 1

1 bulb garlic

2 tablespoons olive oil

3 slices Parma ham

1 skinless, boneless chicken breast

200ml hot chicken stock

100ml double cream

1 tablespoon chopped fresh flat-leaf parsley

1 tablespoon chopped fresh basil

Handful of green beans, steamed, to serve

Salt and freshly ground black pepper

Preheat the oven to 180°C/350°F/gas mark 4. Place the entire bulb of garlic in a square foil with 1 tablespoon of the olive oil. Wrap it up securely and place in the oven for about 30 minutes or until the bulb has softened completely and can be pulled apart and the garlic from each clove can be squeezed out.

Lay the Parma ham slices beside each other, slightly overlapping. Season the chicken breast and place it in the middle of the ham. Fold the slices over the chicken so that it is evenly wrapped.

Heat the remaining olive oil in a frying pan and cook the chicken parcel for 2–3 minutes on each side. Transfer to an ovenproof dish and cook in the oven for a further 15 minutes. Remove from the oven and allow to rest.

In a small pan, reduce the chicken stock by half, add the cream and 3 cloves of roasted garlic. (Keep the rest of the garlic and mix with mayonnaise for a quick garlic mayo.) Reduce by half again and strain. Stir through the chopped herbs.

Serve the steamed beans on a warmed plate, place the chicken on top and spoon the sauce over. Enjoy!

I've dedicated this dish to a fantastic woman called Tina Silvagni, who is my best friend's mother. She always says how much she likes to cook anything with lamb, especially lamb cutlets. Personally this is my favourite cut of lamb. Make sure you marinate the meat for at least thirty minutes and do not overcook the cutlets otherwise they will be quite tough. If you want, you can use the same marinade for pork chops.

Lamb Cutlets Tina-style

Abbacchietti alla Tina SERVES 1

5 lamb rib chops

2 tablespoons olive oil

2 pinches dried chilli flakes

2 tablespoons pitted Kalamata olives, sliced

1 garlic clove, sliced

2 pinches dried oregano

Zest and juice of ½ small unwaxed lemon

Salt and freshly ground black pepper

Use a meat mallet to gently flatten the chops and place them in a large non-metallic bowl. Pour in the oil, add the chilli, olives, garlic, oregano and the lemon zest and juice. Season with salt and turn the chops in the marinade to coat both sides. Leave to marinate at room temperature for 30 minutes.

Once ready, scrape the marinade from the chops, reserving the marinade. Heat a frying pan and cook the chops for 2 minutes on each side until they are beautifully coloured.

Pour the reserved marinade with 2 tablespoons water into the pan and continue to cook the chops over a medium heat for 2 minutes on each side. (This timing will give you medium-rare meat.)

Place the chops on a warm serving plate and pour over the juices from the pan. Serve immediately with a tasty potato salad (see page 51) and a cold beer.

This is what I call the ultimate comfort food. I bet anyone who doesn't like chicken livers that they will absolutely love this dish and you can eat it at any time of the day. The secret is to make sure that you serve it with good-quality breadsticks (see page 142) or warm crusty bread.

Garlic Chicken Liver Pâté with Green Peppercorns

Pate di Fegatini di Pollo all'Aglio e Pepe SERVES 1, FREEZE THE REMAINING 5 PORTIONS

50g salted butter

500g chicken livers, trimmed

⅛ teaspoon dried oregano

4 garlic cloves, crushed

2 tablespoons brandy

1 tablespoon freshly squeezed lemon juice

1 tablespoon green peppercorns in brine, drained and finely chopped

Salt

Melt the butter in a large frying pan and add the livers, oregano and the garlic. Cook over a medium heat for 10 minutes, stirring occasionally.

Pour in the brandy and set alight with a match or lighter. Allow to flame for 5 seconds. Once the flame is out, remove from the heat and stir in the lemon juice. Allow to cool slightly.

Transfer the contents of the pan into a blender or a food processor and blitz until smooth. Season with salt.

Stir the chopped peppercorns into the pâté.

Spoon equally into 6 ramekins, cover with clingfilm and refrigerate for 2 hours.

Buonissimo with homemade cheesy breadsticks (see page 142).

Freeze the remaining pâté in the ramekins for up to 10 days.

I often prepare this dish when I'm on my own, simply because it cooks very quickly. I don't need too many ingredients and the taste is unbelievable. I know that gammon steak is quite an old-fashioned cut of meat but trust me, it will not disappoint, and like everything in life the old-fashioned way is normally the best. You can substitute the gammon steak with a pork chop or chicken breast and if you don't like mascarpone cheese, just use any other soft cheese.

Spicy Gammon Steak with Mascarpone Peas

Bistecca di Pancetta al Peperoncino con Crema di Piselli SERVES 1

2 tablespoons olive oil

2 teaspoons salted butter

½ teaspoon dried chilli flakes

1 tablespoon finely chopped fresh flat-leaf parsley

1 gammon steak (about 180g)

80g frozen peas, defrosted

2 tablespoons mascarpone cheese

Salt and freshly ground black pepper

Heat half the oil and half the butter in a medium frying pan. Add the chilli flakes and half the parsley. Cook the gammon steak for 3 minutes on each side. Transfer to a warm serving plate and pour over the juices from the pan.

Wipe out the pan with some kitchen paper and return to the heat with the remaining oil and butter. Add the peas and cook over a high heat for 2 minutes, tossing continuously.

Season with salt and pepper, add the mascarpone cheese and the remaining parsley. Turn off the heat and use a fork to roughly mash the peas into the mascarpone.

Place the mushy peas next to the gammon steak and serve.

Creamy Rice Pot with Amaretto and Toasted Almonds

Risotto Dolce all'Amaretto e Mandorle SERVES 1

400ml skimmed milk

20g caster sugar

40g Arborio risotto rice

1 teaspoon orange zest

½ teaspoon vanilla extract

1 tablespoon Amaretto liqueur

2 tablespoons skinned almonds

1 teaspoon soft brown sugar

Pour the milk and the caster sugar into a medium saucepan and stir over a low heat until the sugar has dissolved.

Add the rice and orange zest and stir briefly. Bring to the boil then immediately reduce the heat to as low as possible. Cook for 45 minutes, stirring occasionally. Once it looks thick and creamy and the rice is tender, stir in the vanilla extract and the Amaretto liqueur. Set aside to relax for 3 minutes.

Preheat the grill to high.

Meanwhile, dry toast the almonds in a small frying pan for 2 minutes over a medium heat. Shake the pan occasionally. Finely chop the toasted almonds.

Spoon the rice mixture into a cappuccino cup, sprinkle over the toasted almonds then the soft brown sugar.

Grill briefly until the sugar has almost melted. Serve immediately.

Strawberry, Banana and Tarragon Smoothie

Frullato di Fragole e Banana SERVES 1

100g fresh strawberries

1 banana

Leaves from 2 fresh tarragon sprigs

60ml vanilla yogurt

70g ice

Fresh mint leaves, to decorate

Put everything, apart from the mint, into a food processor and blitz until creamy and smooth.

Serve in a tall glass decorated with mint leaves.

If you are looking for a dessert that you are not going to feel really guilty about eating, this is the one to choose. I know that it may sound like a lot of effort to make a meringue, but believe you me, it really is one of the easiest things to prepare. You can substitute the peach with pears and, if they are out of season, just use tinned peach halves.

Marzipan-stuffed Peach with Meringue

Pesca Alaska SERVES 1

1 ripe peach, halved and stone removed

15g marzipan

50g caster sugar

1 large egg white

1 tablespoon Demerara sugar

Preheat the oven to 200°C/400°F/gas mark 6.

Remove the skin from the peach by placing it cut side down on a plate. Put the plate in the sink and pour first boiling water then cold water over it. Drain immediately and peel.

Roll the marzipan into a ball and place in the hollow left by the peach stone, then press the halves back together.

In a large, clean bowl, whisk the egg white until stiff peaks form, gradually add in the caster sugar and continue to whisk until thick and glossy.

Cover the peach completely with a layer of meringue ensuring there are no gaps. Use a fork to rough up the surface of the meringue.

Place the peach in a shallow ovenproof dish, sprinkle with the Demerara sugar and bake in the middle of the oven for 18 minutes until the meringue is lightly browned.

Serve immediately with your favourite ice cream.

Per Tutti I Giorni

Everyday suppers

I could really have written a whole book on

everyday food as it's very much my style of cooking. I don't believe in using fussy cooking methods and strange ingredients. All the recipes in this chapter have been tested for anyone who wants a great meal with amazing flavours any time of the day, any time of the week. There are some of my favourite pasta dishes, which will make your life simple if you need a good meal using straightforward storecupboard ingredients. The recipe that I'm most proud of, however, is my Italian Toad in the Hole, and in my opinion, it's the best one I've ever tried! It's easy, impressive and massively tasty.

As I was brought up in the south of Italy, I have lived on the traditional tomato and basil bruschette, so I decided to try and create other toppings to make this starter or brunch dish even more exciting. I often use this recipe when I have people around for dinner and so far it has never failed to impress. If you are not a big fan of anchovies, you can always use tinned sardines and please make sure you use a good extra virgin olive oil.

Bruschette with Roast Pepper and Cannellini Puree, Black Olive Relish and Rocket

Bruschette SERVES 6 AS A STARTER

8 tablespoons extra virgin olive oil

1 small onion, chopped

1 teaspoon smoked paprika

400g tinned cannellini beans, drained

2 roasted peppers (from a jar)

50g pitted Kalamata olives, chopped

3 tablespoons chopped fresh flat-leaf parsley

1 tablespoon freshly squeezed lemon juice

40g rocket leaves

1 baguette, cut into 2cm thick slices

Salt and pepper to taste

Heat 2 tablespoons of the olive oil in a medium saucepan and fry the onions for 5 minutes stirring occasionally. Add the smoked paprika and cook for 2 more minutes.

Place the onion mixture, beans, roasted peppers and 2 more tablespoons of the olive oil into a food processor and blend until smooth. Season and allow to cool slightly.

To make the black olive relish, place the olives and parsley in a bowl. Pour over the remaining oil and 1 tablespoon lemon juice. Season and stir well.

Place the bread slices on a hot griddle pan and cook for 2 minutes on each side until lightly charred.

To serve, spread some of the cannellini and roast pepper purée over each warm bruschetta and spoon on a little of the olive relish. Top with a few rocket leaves and drizzle with a touch more extra virgin olive oil and place on a large serving plate. Perfect with a cold glass of good Prosecco.

For the first seventeen years of my life I didn't really eat soups except for the odd minestrone once or twice a year but since I've lived in England I have become a convert. This is a great winter warming soup which, served with some fresh warm crusty bread, goes down as one of my favourites. This is one of those dishes that, eaten the day after, is even better than the day you made it.

Chunky Winter Vegetable and Bean Soup

Zuppa di Verdure e Fagioli SERVES 4

6 tablespoons extra virgin olive oil, plus extra for drizzling

1 onion, roughly chopped

2 carrots, peeled and cut into 2cm chunks

2 turnips, cut into chunks

2 celery stalks, roughly chopped

150g curly Savoy cabbage, roughly chopped

1 bay leaf

1.5 litres vegetable stock

400g tinned cannellini beans, drained

150g (prepared weight) pumpkin, cut into 2cm cubes

4 tablespoons roughly chopped fresh flat-leaf parsley

4 slices of rustic country bread

1 garlic clove, cut in half

100g freshly grated Parmesan cheese

Salt and freshly ground black pepper

Heat the olive oil in a large saucepan and fry the onion, carrots, turnips, celery, cabbage and bay leaf until they start to go golden, stirring occasionally.

Pour in the vegetable stock and gently simmer for 30 minutes or until all the vegetables are soft. Stir occasionally.

Add the beans and the pumpkin, and season with salt and pepper. Continue to cook for 15 minutes. Once ready, stir in the parsley and allow to rest for 3 minutes.

Meanwhile, place the bread on a hot griddle pan and cook for about 2 minutes on each side until golden and crispy. Immediately rub with the cut garlic clove and drizzle with some extra virgin olive oil.

To serve, place a slice of bread in each serving bowl and pour over the soup. Sprinkle with Parmesan and serve immediately.

The beautiful thing about this recipe is that you can use it for all different occasions –
starter, breakfast, lunch, main course – anything goes. If you want to, you can substitute
the salmon with rainbow trout and please don't bother making your own fresh mayonnaise
because in this recipe the ready-made one works perfectly. My only serving tip for this dish
is to serve the mousse with some warm crusty bread – amazing!

Fresh Salmon and Lemon Mousse

Mousse di Salmone Fresco SERVES 8

360g piece fresh
salmon (tail end)

1 small onion, sliced

1 carrot, sliced

2 bay leaves

80ml dry white wine

165ml cold water

15ml gelatine sheets

300ml milk

30g salted butter

30g plain flour

5 tablespoons
mayonnaise

Zest of 1 large
unwaxed lemon

160ml double cream

Salt and white
pepper

Place the salmon in a medium saucepan with half the sliced onion
and half the carrot, 1 bay leaf, the white wine and 8 tablespoons of
the water. Season with a little salt, bring to the boil and gently
simmer for 12 minutes.

Transfer the salmon to a plate (reserving the poaching liquid). Remove
and discard the skin using a fork. Flake the fish and place in a bowl.

Boil the reserved liquid until reduced by half, strain and reserve.

Place the gelatine sheets in a bowl and drizzle over the remaining cold
water. Leave to soak for 3 minutes.

Pour the milk into a saucepan and add the remaining onion, carrot
and bay leaf. Bring to the boil and seat aside to infuse for at least
10 minutes. Strain and leave to cool.

Melt the butter in a medium saucepan and stir in the flour. Cook for
1 minute then gradually whisk in the milk. Bring to the boil and
cook for about 10 minutes, whisking continuously, until it thickens.
Pour into a bowl and stir in the soaked gelatine. Leave to cool.

Once ready, pour the white sauce into a blender or food processor
with the flaked salmon and the reserved cooking juices. Blitz for just
a few seconds – you want the salmon to retain a little of its texture.

Transfer the salmon mixture into a large bowl and fold in the
mayonnaise and lemon zest.

Whip the cream in a clean bowl until soft peaks form and then fold
into the salmon mixture.

Spoon the mousse into a soufflé dish or a bowl, cover with clingfilm
and refrigerate for 3 hours, until set.

Leave the mousse at room temperature for 30 minutes before serving.
Scoop out, like ice cream, the mousse on serving plates accompanied
with some warm crusty bread.

It really annoys me that couscous is not used as often as you would use rice or potato because I think it's a great ingredient that cooked in the right way, creates a wonderful dish. I learnt this recipe about five years ago when I was in Sicily and this is my favourite way to use couscous. The peppery flavour of the rocket with the freshness of the lemon is an explosive combination – but always, always, always use freshly squeezed lemon juice.

Rocket and Lemon Couscous

Couscous con Rucola e Limone SERVES 6

250ml olive oil

100ml freshly squeezed lemon juice

500g couscous

8 spring onions, chopped

1 cucumber, deseeded and roughly chopped

130g rocket leaves, roughly chopped

Zest of 1 unwaxed lemon

Salt and freshly ground black pepper

Whisk together the oil and lemon juice in a small bowl, season with salt and pepper and set aside.

Place the couscous in a large bowl and cover with 650ml cold water. Drain and return the couscous into the same bowl. Leave for 10 minutes to allow the grains to swell. Once ready, rake the grains with a fork to remove any lumps.

Place the couscous in a muslin-lined metal colander and steam over a pan of boiling water for 20 minutes. Separate the grains with the fork occasionally to prevent them clumping.

Transfer the couscous to a warmed serving bowl. Stir in the onions, cucumber and rocket leaves. Pour over the lemon dressing, stir well and sprinkle over the lemon zest.

Serve immediately to accompany a meat or fish dish of your choice.

SERVES
4

I'm going to dedicate this recipe to a great friend of mine who also happens to be a fantastic teacher, Professor Graeme Turner. I remember he once invited me to dinner and he promised me that he was going to cook the ultimate Italian risotto. I have to admit that his risotto was good but he did manage to burn himself and use at least four pans to make something that should be done in one pot. So here you have it, mate – hope it makes your risotto life easier!

Risotto with Parma Ham and Vin Santo

Risotto al Vin Santo SERVES 4

5 tablespoons olive oil

1 red onion, finely chopped

2 celery stalks, finely chopped

1.2 litres chicken stock (made from a stock cube if you wish)

300g Arborio rice

350ml Vin Santo (Italian dessert wine, or a good Italian medium white wine)

2 tablespoons chopped fresh flat-leaf parsley

80g salted butter

120g freshly grated Parmesan cheese, plus extra shavings for garnish

8 slices Parma ham

Salt and freshly ground black pepper

Heat the olive oil in a large saucepan and gently fry the onion for about 5 minutes. Add the celery and cook for a further 5 minutes until softened, stirring occasionally.

Meanwhile, bring the stock to a simmer and adjust the seasoning. Keep hot.

Add the rice to the onion pan and stir with a wooden spoon to ensure every grain is coated in oil. Pour in 300ml of the Vin Santo and cook for 3–4 minutes, stirring, until the rice has absorbed almost all the wine.

Start to stir in the hot stock, a ladleful at a time, only adding more stock when the last ladleful has been absorbed. Continue to add the stock and stir until the rice is cooked, which will take about 20–25 minutes.

Remove the risotto from the heat and pour in the remaining Vin Santo. Add in the parsley, butter, the grated Parmesan and stir continuously for 30 seconds until you have created a creamy texture.

Serve the risotto on warmed serving plates, top with the Parma ham and garnish with Parmesan shavings.

Roasted Onions in Rosemary and Balsamic Vinegar

Cipolle Borretane SERVES 4

3 tablespoons olive oil

24 pickling onions, peeled

5 tablespoons balsamic vinegar

2 tablespoons runny honey

1 tablespoon fresh rosemary leaves, stripped from the stalks

Preheat the oven to 180°C/350°F/gas mark 4.

Heat the olive oil in a large frying pan over a medium heat. Add the onions and fry for 5 minutes, stirring continuously with a wooden spoon, until golden all over.

Pour in the vinegar, 100ml water and the honey and continue to cook, stirring, for 5 minutes until the onions are well coated.

Transfer the onions to a roasting tray, stir in the rosemary and roast in the oven for 15 minutes. Shake the tray at least twice during the roasting time.

Remove the onions from the tray, cool to room temperature and serve with other antipasti or as a side dish.

Roasted Aubergines with Red Onions and Goat's Cheese

Melanzane Arrosto SERVES 4

4 garlic cloves, unpeeled

2 large aubergines, cut into 1cm-thick slices

2 red onions, peeled and cut into 4 wedges

5 sprigs fresh thyme

6 tablespoons extra virgin olive oil

150g firm goat's cheese

4 tablespoons roughly chopped fresh flat-leaf parsley

Salt and freshly ground black pepper

Preheat the oven to 190°C/375°F/gas mark 5.

Use the flat side of a knife to squash the unpeeled garlic cloves to release their flavour.

Place the aubergines and the onions in a roasting tray in a single layer. Scatter over the garlic and the thyme. Drizzle with the oil, ensuring that all the aubergines are coated, and season with salt and pepper.

Roast in the middle of the oven for about 30 minutes or until the aubergines are starting to brown around the edges.

Transfer to a large serving dish and crumble over the goat's cheese. Garnish with parsley and serve with a little salad and fresh bread.

Make sure that you always add the goat's cheese and the parsley at the last minute before serving.

I have to admit that I'm not a big fan of curry, probably because it contains too many flavours and I'm not used to it, but whenever I have one, I tend to go for something mild and mainly vegetable based. Cauliflower works perfectly with the flavour of the curry paste and the sweetness of the coconut milk balances the dish beautifully. I've tried this recipe with mixed vegetables and potatoes and it's fantastic.

Cauliflower Curry

Cavolfiore al Curry SERVES 4

3 tablespoons olive oil

2 onions, finely chopped

1cm piece of ginger, peeled and grated

3 tablespoons curry paste

400ml tinned coconut milk

400g tinned chopped tomatoes

1 cauliflower, broken into pieces

2 potatoes, peeled and cut into 2cm chunks

3 tablespoons freshly squeezed lemon juice

200g spinach leaves, washed

Salt to taste

Heat the oil in a large saucepan and fry the onions for 5 minutes over a medium heat until softened, stirring occasionally.

Add the ginger and curry paste and continue to fry for 3 more minutes, stirring continuously.

Pour in the coconut milk and the chopped tomatoes and bring to a simmer. Add the cauliflower and the potatoes and cook for about 25 minutes or until the potatoes are softened. Season with salt.

Remove the saucepan from the heat. Add the lemon juice and spinach, cover, and leave for 2 minutes.

Serve hot just as it is or to accompany one of your favourite main courses.

This is the ultimate boys dish. I absolutely love pulses and I always try to find a different way to cook them. This is a classic for when I have all the boys round to watch *The Godfather* (again!). It gives you a kick, it's tasty and healthy and it's very filling. You can use any kind of pulse you like or, even better, use a mixture of them to get different colours and textures.

Hot and Spicy Chick Peas

Ceci all'Arrabbiata SERVES 4

2 tablespoons olive oil

1 onion, chopped

2 x 400g tins chick peas, drained

2 teaspoons dried chilli flakes

5 large plum tomatoes, skinned and cut into 1cm cubes

5 tablespoons chopped fresh flat-leaf parsley

Salt to taste

Put the oil in a medium saucepan over a moderate heat, and add the onions. Cook for about 8 minutes until golden brown, stirring constantly.

Add the chick peas, the chilli flakes and the tomatoes. Continue to cook for a further 5 minutes. Stir occasionally to prevent it sticking.

Just before serving, season to taste, stir in the parsley and serve hot with your favourite main course.

What can I say... this is definitely a French-style soup. But in my defence, this is such a
simple soup to prepare – and I guess the French do come a close second to us Italians
(sorry Mr Novelli) when it comes to cooking. You can substitute the Gruyére cheese with a
good-quality Cheddar cheese and make sure that you serve this delicious soup in warmed
serving bowls.

Onion Soup with Cheesy Croûtons

Zuppa di Cipolle con Crostini al Formaggio SERVES 2

50g salted butter

250g red onions,
halved and thinly
sliced

1 teaspoon brown
sugar

70ml dry white wine

500ml vegetable
stock

1 bay leaf

1 small sprig fresh
thyme

2 slices country-
style bread
(preferably 4–5 days
old)

50g freshly grated
Gruyère cheese

Salt and freshly
ground black pepper

Melt the butter in a medium saucepan and gently cook the onions
for about 8 minutes until softened, stirring occasionally. Add the
sugar and continue to cook for a further 5 minutes until the onions
begin to caramelise.

Pour in the wine and cook for 1 minute then add the stock, bay leaf
and thyme and simmer for 25 minutes. Stir occasionally and at the
end season with salt and pepper.

Meanwhile, preheat the grill. Place the bread on the grill pan and
scatter over the cheese. Grill for 2–3 minutes until the cheese is
bubbling and golden. Cut each slice into quarters.

Pour the soup into warmed bowls and serve topped with the cheesy
croûtons.

In the last five or six years there has been a new trend in the south of Italy to create dishes with flavours from the sea and flavours from the mountains combined together. To be completely honest, I wasn't sure if this would work, but after trying it, I am convinced. Please make sure that your clams are fresh and, if you can't find them, substitute them with mussels. If Porcini mushrooms are out of season, use chestnut mushrooms.

Pasta with Clams, Rosemary and Porcini Mushrooms

Linguine Mare e Monti SERVES 4

6 tablespoons olive oil

2 garlic cloves, finely sliced

1 tablespoon fresh rosemary leaves stripped from the stalks

½ teaspoon crushed dried chillies

200g fresh Porcini mushrooms, cleaned and thickly sliced

10 cherry tomatoes, halved

1kg small clams, cleaned (discard any broken ones and those that do not close when tapped firmly)

50ml dry white wine

500g dried linguine pasta

2 tablespoons chopped fresh flat-leaf parsley

Salt and freshly ground black pepper

Heat the olive oil in a large deep frying pan, add the garlic, rosemary and the chillies and fry for about 40 seconds over a medium heat. Add the mushrooms and cook for a further 5 minutes, stirring occasionally.

Add the cherry tomatoes, season with salt and cook for 1 minute. Set aside and keep warm.

Meanwhile, heat a large saucepan on a high heat, add the clams and the wine, cover with a lid and cook for 4 minutes until the clams have opened. (Discard any that remain closed.) Tip them into a colander for a few seconds then immediately put them in the frying pan with the mushrooms. Try not to completely drain all the juices from the clams.

Meanwhile, cook the pasta in a large saucepan with plenty of boiling salted water until al dente. Drain thoroughly and pour into the frying pan with the clams and Porcini.

Return the frying pan to the heat, sprinkle with the parsley and toss everything together for a minute. Serve immediately.

In the last couple of years I have received so many letters asking me for a good recipe for a traditional toad in the hole that would be crispy, light and rise well. One day I woke up with a mission – I was going to come up with a perfect but easy recipe that conquers people's fear about preparing this dish. Of course I couldn't go all the way down the traditional road as I wanted to add my own touch to this great British classic. Here you have it – enjoy!

Italian Toad in the Hole with Rosemary and Red Onions

SERVES 4

5 tablespoons sunflower oil

8 good-quality Italian sausages

3 red onions, each one cut into 8 wedges

1 tablespoon fresh rosemary leaves, stripped from the stalks

250g plain flour

½ teaspoon salt

4 eggs, lightly beaten

300ml full-fat milk

Salt and freshly ground black pepper

Preheat the oven to 220°C/425°F/gas mark 7.

Heat 1 tablespoon of the oil in a large frying pan over a medium heat. Start to cook the sausages and the onions with the rosemary for 10 minutes. Turn the sausages and onions regularly until browned. Set aside.

Sift the flour with the salt into a large mixing bowl and make a well in the centre. Add the eggs, milk and a pinch of freshly ground black pepper. Whisk to a smooth batter.

Pour the remaining oil into a medium-sized circular ovenproof dish (about 25cm in diameter) and place in the middle of the oven for 8 minutes to allow the oil to become very hot.

Arrange the sausages and the onions in the hot oil, then pour over the batter. Bake in the middle of the oven for 25–28 minutes until puffed up and golden.

For maximum effect, simply place the toad in the hole in the centre of the table and get your guests to tuck in. And don't forget a good bottle of Italian dry red wine to accompany my dish.

I often find myself in a situation where I don't know what to cook for my young boys and this is always a winner. The comments that I always get from them is that it's very tasty and they absolutely love the crispy topping. You can use any kind of cheese that you like and instead of, or as well as peas, you can add chopped, cooked ham. You can also use small shell pasta or bow-shaped pasta.

The Ultimate Maccheroni Cheese

SERVES 4

300g penne or maccheroni

250ml double cream

100g Red Leicester cheese, grated

100g strong Cheddar cheese, grated

100g Gorgonzola, cut into small chunks

¼ freshly grated nutmeg

2 mozzarella balls, drained and cut into 1cm cubes

3 egg yolks

150g frozen peas, defrosted

100g freshly grated Parmesan cheese

Salt and freshly ground black pepper

Preheat the oven to 220°C/450°F/gas mark 7.

Cook the pasta in a large saucepan with plenty of boiling salted water until al dente. Once the pasta is cooked, drain and place back in the same saucepan away from the heat.

Pour in the cream along with the Red Leicester, Cheddar, and Gorgonzola cheese. Return the saucepan to a low heat and use a wooden spoon to mix everything together for 1 minute.

Remove the pan from the heat and add the nutmeg, the mozzarella, the egg yolks, the peas and half the Parmesan cheese. Season with a little salt, plenty of black pepper and stir everything together for a good 30 seconds.

Tip the mixture into a shallow-sided ovenproof dish (about 30 x 20cm), sprinkle the remaining Parmesan on top and bake in the middle of the oven for about 15 minutes or until it is bubbling and blistering on top.

Serve immediately with your favourite beer.

It is traditional, especially in northern Italy, to serve lamb with polenta, but in this case I think that mashed potato is the ultimate accompaniment – it's impossible to resist the juicy gravy over the mash. I know that as an everyday dinner this recipe may seem extravagant but trust me it is so easy to make and tastes amazing. The secret to get the best results is to use good-quality lamb shanks from your local butcher and a good bottle of red wine. You can substitute the redcurrant jelly with cranberry sauce.

Roasted Lamb Shank in Red Wine Sauce with Italian Mashed Potatoes

Agnello al Vino Rosso con Purée di Patate SERVES 4

4 lamb shanks

1 carrot, cut into chunks

1 white onion, cut into chunks

3 sprigs fresh rosemary

3 sprigs fresh thyme, plus 4 for garnish

10 whole peppercorns

1 bottle of good-quality red wine

3 red onions, quartered

3 tablespoons redcurrant jelly

FOR THE MASH

5 large floury potatoes (such as King Edward), peeled and quartered

150ml full-fat milk

100g salted butter

50g freshly grated Parmesan cheese

100g sun-dried tomatoes in oil, drained and finely chopped

Salt and white pepper

Place the lamb shanks, carrot, white onion, herbs and peppercorns in a large casserole. Pour over the wine, cover and leave to marinate in a cool place for 5 hours, stirring every hour.

When ready to cook, preheat the oven to 190°C/375°F/gas mark 5. Place the casserole on the hob and bring to the boil. Cover with the lid and cook in the oven for 2 hours. For the second hour slightly uncover the casserole to allow the sauce to thicken slightly.

Remove the casserole from the oven, and transfer the lamb shanks from the cooking liquid into a roasting tin. Spoon over 4 ladlefuls of the liquid to keep the meat moist and add the red onions to the tin.

Return the lamb to the oven and roast for 25–30 minutes or until the meat starts to fall off the bone, basting occasionally.

Strain the cooking liquid into a small saucepan and reduce to half its volume on a low heat. Add the redcurrant jelly and stir until melted.

Meanwhile, prepare the mash. Cook the potatoes in plenty of boiling salted water until tender. Drain well and leave to cool slightly.

Press the potatoes through a ricer back into the saucepan, add the milk and return to a low heat. Stir continuously for 3 minutes using a wooden spoon. Add the butter, cheese and sun-dried tomatoes and continue to stir for a further 5 minutes. Season with salt and pepper.

Serve a generous spoonful of the mash in the centre of each serving plate, place the lamb shank on top and drizzle with the delicious redcurrant sauce.

Garnish with a sprig of fresh thyme and serve immediately.

For anybody who isn't a big fan of rich tomato sauces, this has to be the perfect pasta recipe if you still want bags of flavour on your plate. I have chosen three different kinds of meats because the pork will give you a great sweet flavour, the beef is good for texture and the lamb gives you the earthy taste that, combined with the mascarpone cheese, brings the dish together. It's a sauce that you can prepare the day before and if you have any leftover it is fantastic on a jacket potato or rice. You don't have to use all three meats, but try at least to use two and make sure you brown the meat properly before you add the wine.

Rigatoni with White Ragu

Rigatoni al Ragu Bianco SERVES 4

3 tablespoons olive oil

50g salted butter

1 onion, finely chopped

1 celery stick, finely chopped

1 carrot, finely chopped

100g smoked diced pancetta

100g minced pork

100g minced lamb

200g minced beef

150ml white wine

200ml vegetable stock

250g mascarpone cheese

½ teaspoon freshly grated nutmeg

4 tablespoons chopped fresh flat-leaf parsley

500g dried rigatoni pasta

100g freshly grated Pecorino Romano cheese, to serve

Salt and freshly ground black pepper

Heat the olive oil and the butter in a large saucepan and fry the onion, celery, carrot and pancetta for about 10 minutes over a high heat until softened and golden.

Add the pork, lamb and beef and mix well to allow the minced meats to crumble. Cook, stirring frequently, for about 10 minutes or until the meat has browned.

Pour in the wine and cook until evaporated. Season and add the stock. Lower the heat and simmer, uncovered, for 30 minutes, stirring occasionally to prevent it sticking.

Mix in the mascarpone, nutmeg and parsley and allow to rest for 10 minutes.

Meanwhile, cook the pasta in a large saucepan with plenty of boiling salted water until al dente. Once the pasta is cooked, drain thoroughly and add immediately to the sauce. Mix the sauce and the pasta with a wooden spoon over a high heat for about 1 minute.

Serve immediately with plenty of grated Pecorino on top.

If there is one thing I love about British food, it's got to be a good pie. It's shame that not many people cook pies anymore and I'm sure it's because everyone thinks that it's difficult. This is my version of a British pie – every one of my friends who have made this recipe have said how easy it is. You can substitute the cauliflower with broccoli and, if you want to make it more exciting, substitute the carrots with a selection of wild mushrooms.

Italian Vegetable Bake

Sformato di Vegetali SERVES 6

150g carrots, chopped

150g courgettes, chopped

150g cauliflower florets

2 egg whites

30g freshly grated Parmesan cheese

Salt and freshly ground black pepper

FOR THE BÉCHAMEL SAUCE

30g salted butter

30g plain flour

300ml cold milk

¼ teaspoon grated nutmeg

Preheat the oven to 190°C/375°F/gas mark 5.

Bring a large saucepan of salted water to the boil and cook the carrots, courgettes and cauliflower until tender. Drain and allow to cool slightly.

Meanwhile, make the béchamel sauce. Melt the butter in a medium saucepan over a medium heat. Stir in the flour and cook for 1 minute. Gradually whisk in the milk, reduce the heat and cook for 10 minutes, whisking constantly. Once thickened, stir in the nutmeg, season with salt and pepper and set aside to cool slightly.

Place the vegetables in a food processor and blitz to a smooth purée. Pour into a large bowl. Stir the béchamel sauce into the purée.

In a large clean bowl, whisk the egg whites until soft peaks forms and fold into the vegetable mixture.

Pour everything into an ovenproof dish and bake in the middle of the oven for 10 minutes. Sprinkle over the Parmesan and return to the oven for a further 10 minutes.

Serve hot with your favourite salad and accompanied with delicious homemade cheesy breadsticks (see page 142).

This is a recipe that you will find in every Italian cookery book but mine will guarantee maximum satisfaction! You can use ready-made béchamel sauce, but making your own will mean that it tastes that little bit more special and give you a feeling of accomplishment. You can substitute the minced beef with minced lamb and, once ready and out of the oven, make sure that you let it rest for a good 10 minutes, otherwise it will fall apart as you serve it.

The No.1 Lasagna

Lasagna Numero Uno SERVES 6–8

3 tablespoons olive oil

1 onion, finely chopped

1 large carrot, chopped into 1cm cubes

1 celery stalk, finely chopped

500g minced beef

1 glass Italian dry red wine

400g tinned chopped tomatoes

1 tablespoon tomato purée

1 courgette, chopped into 1cm cubes

10 basil leaves

9 sheets fresh lasagna (each about 10 x 18cm)

50g cold salted butter, cut into 1cm cubes

Salt and freshly ground black pepper

FOR THE BÉCHAMEL SAUCE

100g salted butter

100g plain flour

1 litre full-fat cold milk

100g freshly grated Parmesan cheese

¼ freshly grated nutmeg

Heat the olive oil in a large saucepan over a medium heat and cook the onion, carrot and celery for 5 minutes. Add the minced beef and continue to cook for a further 5 minutes, stirring continuously, until coloured all over. Season with salt and pepper and continue to cook for 5 minutes, stirring occasionally.

Pour in the wine, stir well and continue to cook for about 5 minutes until the wine has evaporated.

Add the chopped tomatoes, the tomato purée, the courgettes and the basil, lower the heat and continue to cook for 1 hour, uncovered, until you get a beautiful rich sauce. Stir occasionally. After about 30 minutes, taste for seasoning.

Meanwhile, preheat the oven to 180°C/350°F/gas mark 4, and make the béchamel sauce. Melt the butter in a large saucepan over a medium heat. Stir in the flour and cook for 1 minute. Gradually whisk in the cold milk, reduce the heat and cook for 10 minutes whisking constantly. Once thickened, stir in half of the Parmesan cheese with the nutmeg, season and set aside to cool slightly.

Spread a quarter of the béchamel sauce in the base of a deep 2.2-litre ovenproof dish. Cover with 3 lasagna sheets, cutting them if necessary to fit the dish. Spread with half the meat sauce then top with a third of the remaining béchamel sauce. Cover with 3 more sheets of lasagna and then with the remaining meat sauce. Spread over half of the remaining béchamel sauce. Add a final layer of lasagna sheets and gently spread the rest of the béchamel on top ensuring that the lasagna sheets are completely covered.

Sprinkle with the remaining Parmesan and scatter over the cubed butter. Grind some black pepper over the whole lasagna.

Cook on the lowest shelf of the oven for 30 minutes then place the dish on the middle shelf, raise the oven temperature to 200°C/400°F/gas mark 6 and continue to cook for a further 15 minutes until golden and crispy all over.

To tell you the truth I am such a big fan of bread and butter pudding that I had to create my own version of this great dish. The rum with the chocolate is absolutely divine and with a pinch of cinnamon, it becomes a marriage made in heaven. My only tip for this recipe is to make sure that it rests into the fridge for at least six hours before cooking – this will give you a fantastic soufflé effect when it's ready.

Chocolate and Rum Bread and Butter Pudding

Torta di Pane al Cioccolato SERVES 6

10 slices of good-quality white bread (1cm thick)

150g dark chocolate (70 per cent cocoa solids)

430ml whipping cream

4 tablespoons dark rum

80g salted butter

120g caster sugar

Pinch of cinnamon

3 eggs

Chilled double cream, to serve

Remove the crusts from the bread and cut each slice into 4 triangles.

Place the chocolate, whipping cream, rum, butter, sugar and cinnamon in a large bowl set over a saucepan with simmering water. Be careful not to let the bowl touch the water. Once the butter and chocolate have melted and the sugar is completely dissolved, remove the bowl from the heat and stir to amalgamate the ingredients.

In a separate bowl, whisk the eggs and then pour the chocolate mixture over them and whisk again to blend everything together.

Lightly butter a shallow ovenproof dish measuring about 18 x 23 x 5cm.

Pour about a 1cm layer of chocolate mixture into the base of the dish and arrange half the bread triangles over the chocolate in overlapping rows.

Pour half the remaining chocolate over the bread and arrange the rest of the triangles over that, finishing off with a layer of chocolate. Press the bread gently down so that it is evenly covered with the liquid. Leave to cool.

Cover the dish with clingfilm and place in the fridge for at least 6 hours.

Preheat the oven to 180°C/350°F/gas mark 4.

Remove the clingfilm and bake the pudding in the middle of the oven for 35 minutes – the top will be crunchy and the inside still soft and squidgy.

Remove from the oven, leave to relax for about 5 minutes and serve with plenty of chilled double cream poured all over.

Torta di Pane al Cioccolato

SERVES
6

After having such great feedback from my Plum and Limoncello Tart in my previous book, *Fantastico*, I wanted to create something similar for you citrus lovers out there – I'm sure you'll like this one just as much. I have also tried the same recipe with fresh papaya and it's been a great success. Make sure you always serve the tart at room temperature and never straight from the fridge.

The Best Lemon and Mango Tart

Torta di Limoni e Mango SERVES 6–8

200g plain flour

½ teaspoon salt

130g chilled butter, diced

50g ground almonds

2 tablespoons icing sugar, plus extra for dusting

2 egg yolks

1 egg white, beaten

FOR THE FILLING

200g golden caster sugar

4 eggs

150ml double cream

Grated zest and juice of 2 unwaxed lemons

2 mangoes, peeled and cut into 5mm dice

To make the pastry, place the flour, salt, butter, ground almonds and icing sugar in a food processor and whizz to make fine crumbs. Add 2 tablespoons cold water and the egg yolks and pulse until the mixture comes together to make a firm but moist dough. Wrap in clingfilm and chill for 30 minutes.

Turn out the pastry onto a floured surface and lightly shape into a ball. Roll out and use to line a 20cm fluted flan tin. Chill for at least 30 minutes.

Preheat the oven to 190°C/375°F/gas mark 5.

Line the pastry case with greaseproof paper, fill with baking beans and bake in the middle of the oven for 10 minutes. Lift out the paper, return to the oven and continue to bake for a further 5 minutes until the pastry is dry. Brush the pastry with the beaten egg white and return to the oven for another 5 minutes until the egg white has dried and the pastry is shiny. (Using egg white prevents the pastry going soggy once the filling is poured in.)

Reduce the oven temperature to 150°C/300°F/gas mark 2.

To make the filling, whisk the caster sugar and the eggs until foamy. Beat in the cream with the lemon zest and juice. Arrange the mango cubes on the bottom of the empty tart case and carefully pour over the lemon mixture.

Bake in the middle of the oven for 35–40 minutes until just set. (Don't worry if the filling is wobbly in the centre as it will set as it cools.)

Leave to cool then slip it out of the tin and dust with plenty of icing sugar. Serve at room temperature with crème fraîche.

When you have guests for dinner, have you ever felt that after making an effort on the starter and main course, you really can't be bothered to make a dessert. The answer to this dilemma is simple; either go buy a ready-made one or use this recipe because it's the easiest but tastiest dessert to prepare. You can use any berries that you fancy and, instead of whisky, try a good brandy.

Strawberries and Raspberries Layered with Whisky Cream

Fragole e Lamponi SERVES 6

250g strawberries, hulled and halved

250g raspberries

3 tablespoons whisky

2 tablespoons medium oatmeal

2 tablespoons flaked almonds

350ml double cream

2 tablespoons runny honey

Carefully mix together the strawberries and raspberries in a large bowl. Pour in 2 tablespoons of the whisky, toss the fruit to mix and leave to marinate for about 5 minutes. You will want to reserve a few of the marinated berries for decoration.

Meanwhile, dry-toast the oatmeal and almonds in a small frying pan over a medium heat for about 5 minutes. Once golden and toasted, set aside to cool.

Use an electric whisk to whip the cream into soft peaks. Pour in the honey and the remaining whisky and whip for a further 5 seconds until combined.

Fold half the cooled oatmeal and almonds into the mixture.

Layer the berries and the cream evenly into 6 tall dessert glasses, ending with the cream. Cover the glasses with clingfilm and refrigerate for 2 hours.

To serve, remove the clingfilm, sprinkle with the remaining oatmeal and almonds and decorate with the reserved berries.

Facile Facile

Easy, but impressive recipes

Facile in Italian means easy and this is exactly

what you are going to get in this chapter. I wanted to create dishes which look very impressive but are made effortlessly and with few ingredients. This chapter shows off what Italian food is all about – colours, flavours and great textures. The main reason why I decided to write 'Facile Facile' is because I know that today's lifestyle gives us very little time to spend in the kitchen. However, we all love to entertain, have friends over and show off our cooking ability, so this chapter fits these criteria – and there is very little washing up to do too!

If you love eggs and you fancy something full of flavour, this is an exciting dish to try. It's very colourful and extremely easy to prepare. It is also a wonderful dish that can be eaten cold or the day after as packed lunch for the office. Trust me, your colleagues will be so jealous! You can substitute the feta cheese with goat's cheese and, if you are not a big fan of sun-dried tomatoes, use fresh tomatoes instead.

Baked Omelette with Sun-dried Tomatoes, Rocket and Feta Cheese

Frittata SERVES 6

3 tablespoons extra virgin olive oil

250g leeks, trimmed and finely sliced

100g rocket leaves

100g spinach

100g curly kale, shredded

8 large eggs

3 tablespoons chopped fresh mint leaves

150g Greek feta cheese, crumbled

30g freshly grated Parmesan cheese

50g sun-dried tomatoes in oil, drained and thinly sliced

Salt and freshly ground black pepper

Preheat the oven to 170°C/325°F/gas mark 3.

Heat the oil in a large saucepan over a medium heat and cook the leeks for 10 minutes until soft. Add the rocket, spinach and curly kale to the pan and continue to cook for a further 4–5 minutes until they have wilted down. Transfer the mixture in a large bowl and leave to cool slightly.

Break the eggs into the bowl with the greens and add the mint, feta, Parmesan and sun-dried tomatoes. Season and mix well.

Oil a shallow 20cm cake tin, preferably non-stick. Pour in the mixture and bake in the middle of the oven for about 40 minutes or until just set.

Allow the frittata to rest for 3 minutes before slicing. Serve with a beautiful tomato salad.

The one thing that I have to say about this recipe is that it looks spectacular. I love the combination of parsley and peas, and the fact that in less than 20 minutes you will have a soup that you will never forget. I often make it for dinner with some warm crusty bread and it's really filling. If you are stuck for fresh peas, you can always use good-quality frozen ones, but always, always, always use fresh flat-leaf parsley.

Fresh Pea and Parsley Soup

Zuppa di Piselli e Prezzemolo SERVES 4

Knob of butter

4 shallots, finely chopped

800g fresh peas

1 vegetable stock cube

2 tablespoons chopped fresh flat-leaf parsley

100ml double cream

Salt and white pepper

Melt the butter in a large saucepan over a medium heat and cook the shallots for 5 minutes, stirring occasionally. Add in the peas with 800ml water and the stock cube. Bring to the boil then turn down the heat, add the parsley and simmer, covered, for about 12 minutes for young peas and up to 18 minutes for larger or older peas. Stir occasionally.

When the peas are tender, ladle them into a food processor or blender with a little of the cooking liquid. Purée until smooth.

Return the soup to the pan, pour in half the cream, season and reheat without boiling.

Serve in warm bowls garnished with a drizzle of the remaining cream.

I have to admit that I'm not a great lover of beetroot, probably because I don't particularly like sweet and sour together. This, however, is one of the few ways that I will eat beetroot because it works beautifully with the smoked salmon. If you are a beetroot virgin – here you go, this is the one to try. Make sure that you cook the rostis until they are very crispy.

Beetroot Rosti with Smoked Salmon and Horseradish Cream

Crocchette di Barbabietola e Salmone SERVES 4

2 large potatoes
(about 450g),
unpeeled (Maris
Piper are best)

1 beetroot, peeled
and coarsely grated

1 garlic clove,
crushed

5 tablespoons olive
oil

4 slices good-quality
smoked salmon

1 lime, cut into
4 wedges

FOR THE HORSERADISH CREAM

100g mascarpone

Juice of ⅛ lime

2 tablespoons
horseradish sauce

Salt and freshly
ground black pepper

Fresh dill sprigs to
garnish

Put the potatoes into a large saucepan, cover with cold water and bring to the boil. Cook for 12 minutes then drain and leave to cool.

Peel the cooled potatoes and grate into a large bowl. Add the beetroot and the garlic, season and mix well.

Divide and mould the mixture into 4 patties. Leave to chill in the fridge for 40–60 minutes.

Meanwhile, mix the mascarpone, the lime juice and the horseradish in a bowl. Season with salt and plenty of black pepper.

Heat the oil in a frying pan and cook the rostis for about 5 minutes on each side until crisp and golden all over. Remove and drain on kitchen paper.

Place a hot rosti on each serving plate topped with some smoked salmon, a dollop of horseradish cream and a sprig of dill. Place a wedge of lime on the side and serve immediately.

If you like traditional pesto made with basil, oil and pine kernels, you will absolutely love my parsley and caper pesto. This is one of my signature dishes that never fails to impress people and, funnily enough, like all the best dishes in the world, it's very simple to prepare. Please make sure that your pasta is al dente and, once the pasta is mixed into the sauce, you must serve immediately otherwise it will get sticky and soggy. Buon Appetito!

Pasta with Walnut and Caper Pesto

Tagliolini al Pesto di Noci e Capperi SERVES 4

FOR THE PESTO

2 garlic cloves, chopped

80g walnut halves, chopped

2 tablespoons salted capers, rinsed and chopped

50g fresh flat-leaf parsley, chopped

180ml extra virgin olive oil

50g salted butter, softened

5 tablespoons freshly grated Pecorino Romano cheese

Salt and freshly ground black pepper

500g tagliolini (fresh or dried)

Place the garlic, walnuts, capers and a little salt in a pestle and mortar and pound until broken up. Add the parsley and continue to pound until you create a paste. (If you don't have a pestle and mortar, briefly pulse the ingredients in a food processor to a rough pesto.)

Transfer the mixture into a bowl and gradually mix in the oil until creamy and thick. Beat in the butter and season with pepper. Finally beat in the Pecorino.

Meanwhile, cook the pasta in a large saucepan in plenty of boiling salted water until al dente. Drain and return to the pan off the heat.

Pour the pesto in the pan and use a wooden spoon to fold the pesto into the pasta for at least 30 seconds to ensure that the pasta is well dressed. If you like, sprinkle over with a little extra grated Pecorino. Serve immediately with a cold beer.

SERVES

4

This recipe reminds me of Roma, especially around Easter time, because it seems to me that every Roman eats broad beans with Pecorino cheese during the festive season. I personally think that it's a brilliant salad combination because I adore the saltiness of the speck with the sweetness of the broad beans. A simple, tasty dish that can be eaten on its own, or to accompany any meat main course.

Pecorino and Broad Bean Salad with Speck

Insalata di Fave, Pecorino e Speck SERVES 4

12 slices speck
(or prosciutto)

350g fresh broad
beans

6 small celery
stalks, sliced into
5cm long
matchsticks

10 mint leaves,
roughly sliced

100g rocket leaves

5 tablespoons extra
virgin olive oil

Juice of 1 small
lemon

150g Pecorino
Romano cheese,
shaved

Salt and freshly
ground black pepper

Bring a large saucepan of water to the boil and cook the broad beans for no longer than 2 minutes. Drain, rinse in cold water and leave to cool.

Put the beans, celery, mint and rocket leaves in a large bowl. Make a dressing by pouring the oil and lemon juice into a small bowl, season and whisk until it begins to thicken slightly. Pour the dressing over the salad and toss to ensure all the ingredients are well coated.

Share out the salad between four serving plates and fold 3 slices of speck on top of each serving. Scatter the Pecorino shavings over the salads and serve immediately with good, country-style warm bread.

If you asked me the three things I miss most about Italy, my answer would be very simple: the sun, good football and simple and tasty dishes like this one. Unfortunately I don't see enough restaurants serving fresh fish like this and this is such a shame because I'm sure that everybody would love it. This way of marinating and cooking fish in lemon juice is also a traditional Mexican style which relies completely on fresh and good-quality ingredients.

Sea Bass Carpaccio with Chilli and Cherry Tomatoes

Carpaccio di Spigola e Pomodorini di Collina SERVES 4 AS A STARTER

1kg whole sea bass (or salmon if you prefer), filleted

10 cherry tomatoes, halved

5 tablespoons freshly squeezed lemon juice

3 tablespoons extra virgin olive oil

½ teaspoon dried chilli flakes

3 tablespoons fresh oregano leaves

Salt

Place the sea bass fillets on a chopping board, skin side down. Use a long-bladed sharp knife to cut as finely as you can along the length of the fillet. Discard the skin.

Place the fillets, side by side, on a large cold serving plate. Squeeze the juice and the pulp from the halved tomatoes over the fish and scatter the skins on top. Drizzle with the lemon juice and the oil. Season with a little salt and the chilli flakes and scatter with the oregano leaves.

Cover the plate with clingfilm and chill for about 1 hour until the fish is opaque.

Serve with some warm crusty bread of your choice.

Stuffed Roasted Tomatoes with Goat's Cheese and Mozzarella

Pomodori Imbottiti al Formaggio SERVES 6

6 beef tomatoes

125g ball mozzarella cheese, drained and finely chopped

2 tablespoons crushed walnuts

180g goat's cheese, rind removed

2 tablespoons chopped fresh basil

6 thick slices white bread

Extra virgin olive oil, for drizzling

Salt and freshly ground black pepper

Preheat the oven to 190°C/375°F/gas mark 5.

Using a sharp knife, cut a thin slice from the bottom of each tomato, so that the base is flat and the tomatoes won't topple over, and discard. Cut a 1cm thick slice from the top of the tomato, but do not discard. Carefully scoop out the seeds and most of the pulp with a teaspoon, keeping the tomato shells whole.

Mix together the mozzarella, walnuts, goat's cheese and basil. Season with salt and pepper and spoon into the tomato shells. Replace the tomato lid.

Use an 8cm-round pastry cutter to stamp out 6 rounds from the bread slices and toast on both sides. Set aside.

Place the tomatoes on a lightly oiled baking tray and cook in the middle of the oven for about 20 minutes, just until the cheese mixture looks melted and golden (you don't want the tomatoes to be too soft). Serve immediately, on top of the toasted bread, with a little drizzle of extra virgin olive oil on top.

Lentils and Nuts with Chive and Sherry Vinegar Dressing

Lenticchie e Noci con Erba Cipollina SERVES 4

400g tinned green lentils

3 tablespoons walnuts, chopped

2 tablespoons pine kernels, toasted

2 tablespoons chopped hazelnuts

3 tablespoons chopped fresh chives

3 tablespoons extra virgin olive oil

2 tablespoons sherry vinegar

Salt and white pepper

Drain and rinse the lentils under cold water and place in a large bowl. Add the nuts and chives and mix everything together.

Pour in the oil, the vinegar and season with salt and pepper. Toss well and serve with your favourite main course or as a starter with some warm crusty bread.

In my home town, Torre del Greco the words 'scue scue' means something done 'quickly quickly'. This has to be the most tasty, colourful and easy salad that you will ever prepare and will make a good brunch alternative or an easy dinner for any day of the week. My tip is to dress the salad just before serving, otherwise you will cook the lettuce and everything will go dark and soggy.

Quick Ham and Emmental Salad with Dijon Mustard Dressing

Insalata Scue' Scue' SERVES 4

1 head iceberg lettuce, leaves separated and roughly torn

50g radicchio leaves

80g Emmental cheese, grated

150g ham, cut into 1cm cubes

1 ripe avocado, cut into big chunks

200g tinned sweetcorn, drained

4 eggs, boiled for 6 minutes, peeled and quartered

FOR THE DRESSING

4 tablespoons extra virgin olive oil

1 teaspoon Dijon mustard

1 tablespoon red wine vinegar

Salt and freshly ground black pepper

First make the dressing by whisking together the oil, vinegar and mustard in a small bowl and season with salt and pepper.

Place the torn lettuce leaves in a large bowl with the radicchio leaves. Add the cheese, ham, avocado and sweetcorn. Pour in the dressing and toss.

Divide the salad between 4 serving plates and arrange 4 wedges of egg on top.

Serve immediately as a starter or brunch with some warm crusty bread.

I don't about know you, but I sometimes get bored of always having potatoes with my main meal. I created this in order to still have a substantial side dish, but with more exciting colours and flavours. Try this recipe with pumpkin when it is in season and you can use Parmesan cheese instead of Pecorino.

Roasted Squash with Chilli and Sage Crumbs

Zucca al Forno con Peperoncino e Salvia SERVES 6

100g fresh
breadcrumbs

6 tablespoons olive
oil

2 butternut squash,
unpeeled, seeds and
fibres removed, cut
into thin wedges

1 medium hot red
chilli, deseeded and
sliced

2 garlic cloves,
sliced

10 whole fresh sage
leaves

4 tablespoons
freshly grated
Pecorino Sardo

Salt and freshly
ground black pepper

Preheat the oven to 200°C/400°F/gas mark 6.

Put the breadcrumbs in a bowl and drizzle over half the oil. Season with salt and pepper and toss together.

Place the squash in a roasting tray, drizzle with the remaining oil and sprinkle with the chilli, garlic and sage. Season with salt.

Sprinkle over the breadcrumbs and the cheese and bake in the middle of the oven for about 40–45 minutes until tender and golden. Serve hot.

I'm going to dedicate this recipe to my sister Marcella because every time she comes to visit me in London, she always asks me to prepare it. I think the main reason for this is because we don't get good-quality potatoes in Italy; also the flavour of the chives and the cheeses work wonderfully together. Try substituting the Cheddar cheese with Red Leicester and if you want, add a couple of teaspoons of English mustard.

Cheesy Mash with Chives

Purée di Patate con Erba Cipollina SERVES 4

1kg potatoes (King
Edward are best),
peeled and
quartered

150ml full-fat milk

100g freshly grated
Parmesan cheese

50g freshly grated
Cheddar cheese

100g salted butter

5 tablespoons finely
chopped fresh chives

Salt and white
pepper

Put the potatoes into a large saucepan, cover with cold water and bring to the boil. Cook until tender. Drain and mash in the saucepan. Return the pan to a low heat and, using a wooden spoon, stir in the milk then beat to a creamy texture.

Add the cheeses, butter and the chives, season and stir for a further 3 minutes over a low heat until the cheeses are completely melted; you want to create a beautiful creamy texture. Serve immediately.

Pasta is definitely the ultimate Italian fast food. I don't think I've ever met anyone who doesn't like a plate of good pasta. I often make white sauce with mascarpone cheese and this is without doubt one of my top five pasta dishes. The crispness of the pancetta with the sweet peas and the cheese is an explosion of taste. You can substitute the tagliatelle with fusilli or rigatoni and remember: put the pasta into the sauce, never the sauce on top of the pasta!

Pasta with Mushrooms, Peas and Mascarpone

Tagliatelle al Mascarpone SERVES 4

1 tablespoon olive oil

50g salted butter

100g pancetta, cubed

150g button mushrooms, quartered

150g defrosted frozen or fresh peas

250g mascarpone

500g fresh tagliatelle

50g freshly grated Parmesan cheese

Salt and freshly ground black pepper

Heat the oil and butter together in a large frying pan over a medium heat. Add the pancetta and a pinch of black pepper and fry for about 3 minutes until golden.

Add the mushrooms and peas and continue to cook for 8 minutes, stirring occasionally.

Stir in the mascarpone and remove the pan from the heat.

Meanwhile, cook the pasta in a large saucepan with plenty of boiling salted water (for 500g pasta allow at least 3 litres water) until al dente.

Once the pasta is cooked, drain thoroughly and add to the frying pan with the sauce.

Put the pan back on the heat, sprinkle half of the Parmesan over the pasta and toss everything together for a good minute.

Serve immediately, sprinkled with the remaining grated Parmesan.

The original topping for a traditional Neapolitan pizza is tomato, garlic, oregano and extra virgin olive oil. The mozzarella was added by a Neapolitan pizza guy, who wanted to impress a queen called Margherita. Since then it's become probably the most renowned and popular pizza in the world! As you can see I have added a few extra ingredients to make it more exciting so you can do exactly the same as long as it's not pineapple – what is that all about?

Pizza Vesuvio

MAKES 2 PIZZAS

FOR THE DOUGH

Pinch of salt

1 teaspoon dried yeast

140ml warm water

180g strong plain flour, plus extra for dusting

1 tablespoon extra virgin olive oil, plus extra for greasing

FOR THE TOPPING

400g passata (sieved tomatoes)

2 mozzarella balls, cut into pieces (do not use buffalo mozzarella because it is too milky and will make the dough soggy)

12 slices good-quality Italian salame

100g pitted Kalamata black olives, halved

4 tablespoons extra virgin olive oil

30g freshly grated Parmesan cheese

10 fresh basil leaves

Salt and freshly ground black pepper

To make the dough, mix together the salt, yeast and water in a jug. Sift the flour into a large bowl, make a well in the centre and add the yeast mixture along with the olive oil. Use a wooden spoon to mix everything together to create a wet dough.

Turn out the dough onto a clean well-floured surface and work it with your hands for about 5 minutes or until smooth and elastic. Place in a bowl and cover with a tea towel. Leave in a warm place to rest for at least 30 minutes or until the dough almost doubles in size.

Preheat the oven to 220°C/425°F/gas mark 7.

Once rested, turn out the dough onto a floured surface, and divide it into two. Use your hands (or a rolling pin) to push each out from the centre, creating two round discs about 25cm in diameter. Place the pizza bases on two oiled baking trays.

Spread the passata over the pizza dough using a tablespoon and season with salt and pepper. Divide the mozzarella, salame and olives between the pizzas and drizzle with the extra virgin olive oil. Cook in the middle of the oven for about 20 minutes or until golden and brown. Two minutes before the end of the cooking time sprinkle the pizzas with Parmesan and scatter the basil leaves on top.

Serve hot and enjoy with a cold beer.

This is a great recipe that I learned in the town of Sorrento about twenty years ago when I was a student. The secret for this recipe is to buy good-quality lamb and also good-quality juicy lemons. I absolutely adore lamb especially when it's slow cooked and falling off the bone. Ask your butcher to cut the shoulder of lamb through the bone into 4 large chunks. A fantastic recipe that you can prepare in advance and is even better if served the next day.

Slow-Roasted Shoulder of Lamb with Lemon Potatoes

Agnello e Patate al Forno all'Origano e Limone SERVES 4

1.5kg shoulder of lamb

1.5kg waxy potatoes (such as Desirée), peeled and cut into 6cm chunks

10 garlic cloves, unpeeled

1 tablespoon dried oregano

2 tablespoons fresh marjoram leaves

2 tablespoons fresh rosemary leaves, stripped from the stalk

3 bay leaves

5 tablespoons extra virgin olive oil

Juice of 2 large lemons

Salt and freshly ground black pepper

Preheat the oven to 190°C/375°F/gas mark 5.

Place the meat, potatoes and garlic in a large ovenproof casserole dish. Sprinkle in all the herbs and pour in the olive oil, lemon juice and 100ml cold water.

Season with plenty of salt and pepper and mix well together (try to nestle the pieces of meat down among the potatoes.) Cover the casserole dish with foil and a well-fitting lid.

Bake in the middle of the oven for 3 hours until the meat is falling off the bone. Check after about 2 hours to see whether it needs a little more water.

At the end of cooking, let the casserole rest for 10 minutes out of the oven with the lid off.

Serve with plain rice or a fresh salad of your choice.

Originally I wanted to put this recipe in the *Romantico* chapter because it's delicate and very pretty, but then considering how easy it is to prepare, I put it here. I am obsessed with veal and this has to be one of my favourite ways to cook it. The sharpness of the lemon with the sweetness of veal is buonissimo! My tip is to only use fresh sage leaves and never the dried ones from the jars and open a good bottle of cold Italian white wine to serve with this dish.

Veal with Butter, Sage and Lemon Sauce

Scaloppine di Vitello al Limone SERVES 4

3 lemons

30g plain flour, for dusting

4 x 180g thinly sliced veal escalopes

60g salted butter

3 tablespoons extra virgin olive oil

100ml dry white wine

5 fresh sage leaves, finely sliced

Salt and freshly ground black pepper

Peel I lemon and slice into 8 thin slices, without any pith.

Spread the flour on a flat plate, season with salt and pepper and mix.

Dust the veal in the seasoned flour, shaking off any excess.

Melt the butter in a large frying pan over a medium heat then pour in the oil. When it is hot, lay the scaloppine in the pan with the lemon slices and cook for 2 minutes on each side.

Pour in the juice from I½ lemons and the wine and shake the pan constantly – this will make the sauce creamy. Remove the veal and the lemon slices and arrange on a warm serving plate.

Add the sage to the sauce, give it a good shake and pour immediately over the scaloppine.

Serve with a chilled glass of good white Italian wine.

This is my grandmother, nonna Assunta's signature dish. She knows very well that every time I go to see her I expect to see these beautiful meatballs on a plate even if I go there for breakfast. Make sure you use plenty of freshly grated Parmesan cheese and once they are ready you can toss some freshly cooked spaghetti with it.

Neapolitan Spicy Meatballs in Tomato Sauce

Polpette alla Napoletana SERVES 4

500g minced beef

100g salame Napoli, chopped

3 garlic cloves, crushed

70g fresh white breadcrumbs

1 teaspoon dried chilli flakes

3 tablespoons chopped fresh flat-leaf parsley

100g freshly grated Parmesan cheese

1 egg

2 x 720g bottles of passata (sieved tomatoes)

10 fresh basil leaves

4 tablespoons olive oil

Salt and white pepper

Combine the minced beef, salame, garlic, breadcrumbs, chilli flakes, parsley and Parmesan in a large bowl. Season with salt and break in the egg. Mix all the ingredients thoroughly with your hands then shape into 8 balls. Place on a plate and leave in the fridge for 20 minutes.

Meanwhile, pour the passata into a large saucepan and place over a medium heat. Season with salt and pepper, add the basil leaves, bring to the boil then remove from the heat.

Heat the oil in a large frying pan and fry the meatballs for about 5 minutes until golden brown all over.

Place the meatballs in the tomato sauce and continue to cook on a low heat for 1 hour with the pan half covered. Stir occasionally and, if the sauce gets too thick, add a little water.

Serve 2 meatballs per person with the sauce and some freshly cooked pasta or plain rice.

If you decide to prepare a fishy starter and want to follow it with a meat dish, the problem that you will find is that during the main course you will still be able to taste the fish. Well, I have the solution – serve my granita just after the starter and it will cleanse your palate ready for the main course. A fantastic, refreshing sorbet that is also great on a hot day with a barbecue.

Limoncello and Lime Granita

Granita al Limoncello SERVES 4

Zest and juice of
2 limes

1 litre cold water

80g caster sugar

300ml Limoncello
liqueur

Place the lime juice in a medium saucepan with the cold water. Add the sugar and half the lime zest and gently heat until the sugar has dissolved, stirring occasionally.

Remove from the heat, mix in the Limoncello, and leave to cool.

Pour the cooled mixture into a flat freezerproof container and freeze until crystals form around the edges (about 30 minutes, depending on your freezer). At this point, stir the mixture vigorously with a fork then put it back in the freezer.

Repeat this process every 20 minutes over the next few hours until no liquid remains in the container. The consistency you're after is just crunchy with broken crystals of ice.

Serve the granita in tall glasses, decorated with the remaining lime zest.

Not only do my boys Rocco and Luciano love to eat this dessert but they also love to help me make it. This Tiramisu was especially designed for children so of course there is no alcohol involved but if you want a grown-up version, you can always add four or five tablespoons of Amaretto liqueur into the cream mixture. Remember not to soak the biscuits too much otherwise they will get too soggy, and make sure your chocolate is cold.

Chocolate Tiramisu

Tiramisu alla Rocco SERVES 4

6 tablespoons drinking chocolate powder

300ml semi-skimmed milk

300ml whipping cream

250g mascarpone cheese

3 tablespoons caster sugar

1 teaspoon vanilla extract

20 Savoiardi biscuits (lady fingers)

4 chocolate flakes to decorate

Put the drinking chocolate and the milk in a medium saucepan over a medium heat, stirring occasionally. When the chocolate has dissolved, pour into a bowl and leave to cool.

Whip the cream in a large bowl until soft peaks form. Add the mascarpone, sugar and vanilla extract and whisk for a further 10 seconds until everything is combined.

You will need four glass dessert dishes, about 8cm in diameter and 6cm deep.

Dip 8 Savoiardi biscuits into the chocolate milk for 2 seconds on each side and place 2 fingers on the base of each dish. (Break the biscuits to make sure that the bottom of the dish is covered.)

Share out half of the mascarpone cream between the four dishes to cover the fingers.

Dip the remaining biscuits in the chocolate and this time place 3 biscuits on top of the cream in each dish. Finish by smothering the remaining cream over the sponge fingers. Cover each dish with clingfilm and chill for 1 hour.

To serve, remove the clingfilm and sprinkle the chocolate flakes over each Tiramisu.

If you take away the Amaretto liqueur from this recipe, it will be perfect for when you have kids coming over. I guarantee you that everyone is going to love this crispy, chocolatey and chewy little crunchy bars that goes perfectly with a cup of tea or, for the adults, a good brandy. Made sure you use a good-quality chocolate and that the pistachio nuts are not salted.

Chocolate and Pistachio Crunch Bars

Bocconcini di Cioccolato e Pistacchio SERVES 8 (MAKES 24 PIECES)

50g salted butter

300g good-quality dark chocolate (70 per cent cocoa solids), broken into pieces

3 tablespoons golden syrup

3 tablespoons Amaretto liqueur

200g Rich Tea biscuits

80g mini marshmallows

80g crushed pistachio nuts

Icing sugar, for dusting

Place the butter, chocolate, syrup and Amaretto liqueur in a heavy-based saucepan and gently heat until melted. Pour 150ml of the mixture out of the pan and set aside.

Place the biscuits into a large bowl and crush into rough crumbs with your hands. Fold into the chocolate mixture in the saucepan, along with the marshmallows and pistachio nuts.

Pour the mixture into a foil tray measuring about 25cm square, and use a spatula to flatten as best you can. Pour over the reserved melted chocolate and smooth the top.

Cover with clingfilm and refrigerate for about 3 hours or overnight.

To serve, push out the cake on a chopping board and cut into 24 fingers. Dust with icing sugar and place on a large serving dish.

Buonissimo with a good cup of your favourite tea.

I know that this may sound very strange to you, using black pepper in a white chocolate mousse, but believe you me, this is a dessert that all your friends will talk about. This recipe has been designed specifically for this chapter; it's easy, very tasty and definitely has the wow factor, but make sure you use a good-quality chocolate. You can also serve it straight from the freezer like a semi-freddo.

White Chocolate Mousse with Black Pepper and Fresh Mint

Mousse di Cioccolato Bianco e Pepe Nero SERVES 6

280g white chocolate, broken into pieces

300ml double cream

1 tablespoon freshly ground black pepper

12 fresh mint leaves (6 finely sliced, 6 reserved for decoration)

Put the chocolate in a heatproof bowl and place over a pan of simmering water to melt. Make sure the base of the bowl does not touch the water. When the chocolate has melted, stand the bowl on a cold surface to cool down slightly.

Pour the cream into a large bowl and whisk until soft peaks form.

Place 2 tablespoons of cream in the melted chocolate and gently fold together, then fold the chocolate mixture into the rest of the cream. At the end, gently fold in the black pepper and the chopped mint.

Share the mixture between six tall Champagne glasses (capacity of about 70ml).

Chill in the fridge for about 20 minutes, then serve decorated with the reserved mint leaves.

SERVES
6

Salute
Party food for sharing

Whenever I am in Italy and everyone clinks

glasses and shouts out *Salute* (cheers), I know that it's party time. I personally believe that when there is a special occasion, people shouldn't spend too much time in the kitchen preparing things that will take them away from their guests. So here I've created recipes which you can definitely prepare ahead, leaving you plenty of time to party. Take, for example, my semi freddo all'amaretto, a fantastic dessert that, prepared the day before, will taste ten times better. Remember a great party always needs a good drink, so use the one I've suggested to impress your friends. One important tip I can give you is to try the recipe you choose for your party at least once before the big day to make sure that it's going to work perfectly.

Campari Served with Parmesan Crisps

Marco on the Rock SERVES 4

130ml Campari

250ml orange juice

250ml tomato juice

TO SERVE

Ice cubes

Fine strips of
cucumber

FOR THE CRISPS

50g freshly grated
Parmesan cheese

Leaves from 4 fresh
thyme sprigs

First prepare the crisps. Preheat the oven to 180°C/350°F/gas mark 4.
Make 8 small heaps of the grated Parmesan on a baking sheet,
spaced about 2cm apart. Sprinkle the thyme over the cheese piles.
Bake in the oven for 4–5 minutes until melted, lacy and golden.
Remove from the oven and immediately lay each crisp on a rolling
pin to curve it slightly. Set aside to cool.

Meanwhile, mix together the Campari, the orange and the tomato
juices in a large jug. Place several ice cubes in 4 glasses, then pour
over the mixed Campari. Decorate the glass with the cucumber strips
and enjoy with your Parmesan crisps.

Cheesy Breadsticks with Pecorino Cheese and Thyme

Grissini al Pecorino MAKES 35–40

20g dried yeast

300ml tepid milk

750g strong white
plain flour, plus
extra for dusting

20g salt

60g freshly grated
Pecorino cheese

100g salted butter at
room temperature

Extra virgin olive
oil, for greasing

2 tablespoons finely
chopped fresh thyme
leaves, stripped from
the sprigs

Mix the yeast in a glass with 3 tablespoons of the milk, stir well and
leave to rest for 10 minutes.

Stir the flour, salt and cheese together in a large bowl. Rub in the
butter using your fingertips until the mixture resembles breadcrumbs.
Stir in the yeast mixture and gradually incorporate the remaining
milk to form a soft dough.

Turn out the dough onto a floured surface and knead for about
10 minutes until the dough is soft and elastic.

Lightly oil a large bowl and place the dough in it. Drizzle the top
with a little more oil and cover with clingfilm. Leave in a warm
place for about 1 hour until nearly doubled in size.

Once the dough is ready, knock it back by punching it, then turn
out on a clean unfloured surface. Cut into 8 pieces, roll out, then
cut each into sausage shapes about 1.5cm thick and the length of
a baking tray. Sprinkle over the chopped thyme and divide them
between 2 baking trays. Leave to rest for 15 minutes in a warm place.
Meanwhile, preheat the oven to 240°C/450°F/gas mark 8.

Bake the breadsticks in the middle of the oven for about 15 minutes
until golden. Leave to cool on a wire rack. Serve them warm or cold.

I designed this recipe on the day that my son Luciano turned six. I remember my wife saying that the food she was going to prepare was a little boring, so she asked me to come up with something more exciting. This turned out to be the highlight of the birthday. I think the only problem I had was that I did not prepare enough, so my only tip is to make sure that you have plenty because everyone will love it.

Stuffed Focaccia with Spinach, Olives and Mozzarella

Focaccia Farcita SERVES 6

450g strong plain white flour

2 teaspoons dried yeast

4 tablespoons extra virgin olive oil, plus extra for brushing

300ml warm water

250g frozen spinach, defrosted

200g mozzarella cheese, chopped

4 tablespoons pitted Kalamata olives, chopped

2 teaspoons fresh thyme leaves, stripped from the sprigs

Maldon sea salt for sprinkling

Salt and freshly ground black pepper

Sift the flour into a large bowl and stir in the yeast. Make a well in the centre, pour in the oil and the water and with the help of a wooden spoon, mix all together.

Transfer the mixture on a floured surface and knead for 10 minutes until the dough is smooth and elastic.

Place the dough into a greased bowl, cover with a clean tea-towel and leave to rise in a warm place for about 1½ hours until nearly doubled in size.

Meanwhile, squeeze the defrosted spinach to remove any excess water and place in a large bowl. Add the mozzarella, the olives and the thyme. Season with salt and pepper and mix well.

Preheat the oven to 220°C/425°F/gas mark 7. Brush a 25cm loose-based cake tin with oil.

Knock back the dough by punching it, and divide it into two pieces. Roll out the first piece a little larger than the tin. Place on the bottom of the tin and mould the sides to be higher than the base.

Spread the spinach mixture over the base to within 1cm of the edge.

Roll out the remaining dough to the size of the tin, brush the edges with a little water and place over the filling. Press the edges together to ensure a good seal.

Using your fingers, press all over the surface and then brush with the extra virgin olive oil. Sprinkle with the Maldon salt and bake in the middle of the oven for 30 minutes until risen and firm.

Remove the focaccia from the oven and allow to rest in the tin for 10 minutes then place on a wire rack to slightly cool. Enjoy while still warm and fragrant. If you do have any leftover, it will still taste great for lunch the next day.

I absolutely love tarts and it's a shame that not many people cook them anymore, maybe because it is thought to be quite a difficult dish to prepare. Some of my friends have tried this dish and they say that it's definitely one of the easiest and tastiest tart recipes that they have ever made. I often choose this kind of recipe when I have a dinner party because if there is any left over, I'll take it to my office and have it cold for lunch with some salad.

Artichoke and Spinach Tart

Torta di Carciofi e Spinaci SERVES 8

3 tablespoons olive oil

2 onions, thinly sliced

8 artichokes hearts in oil from a jar, drained and halved

400g ready-made shortcrust pastry

Flour for dusting

400g baby spinach leaves, roughly chopped

6 eggs

50g freshly grated Parmesan cheese

80g feta cheese, crumbled

Salt and freshly ground black pepper

Preheat the oven to 180°C/350°F/gas mark 4.

Heat the olive oil in a large frying pan over a medium heat and fry the onions for 5–6 minutes until softened, stirring occasionally. Add the artichokes with 80ml water, cover the pan, and braise over a gentle heat for 6 minutes.

Roll out the pastry on a lightly floured surface and use to line a 25cm loose-based tart tin. Chill in the freezer for 10 minutes.

Line the tart tin with baking paper and baking beans, place on a baking tray and cook in the middle of the oven for 15 minutes. Remove the paper and beans and set aside to cool.

Meanwhile, blanch the spinach by putting it in a colander over the sink and pouring boiling water over it. Squeeze out the excess water and set aside.

Lightly beat the eggs in a large bowl, add in the cheeses and spinach. Season and mix well then stir in the artichokes and onions.

Pour the mixture into the pastry case and spread out evenly. Place in the middle of the oven and bake for about 30 minutes or until the filling is just set.

Allow the tart to cool in the tin for 15 minutes, then remove and transfer to a large plate.

Cut into slices and serve warm with your favourite salad.

This is the ultimate Neapolitan recipe. I still remember my teenage years when I rode around on my scooter with my friends and stopped off in a pizzeria for a quick calzone. I've given a meat and a vegetarian filling here but, of course, you can stuff them with almost anything you want – for example, you can substitute the cooked ham with cooked bacon or Parma ham. Don't prepare this recipe in advance because the filling will make the dough soggy.

Calzone

MAKES 6

FOR THE DOUGH

2 pinches of salt

2 teaspoons dried yeast

280ml warm water

360g strong plain flour, plus extra for dusting

2 tablespoons extra virgin olive oil, plus extra for greasing

FOR THE VEGETARIAN FILLING

500g ricotta cheese

80g freshly grated Pecorino cheese

100g rocket leaves, chopped

80g pistachios, crushed

Pinch of freshly grated nutmeg

4 tablespoons extra virgin olive oil

FOR THE MEAT FILLING

100g pesto

6 slices cooked ham

6 slices mozzarella

Salt and freshly ground black pepper

To prepare the dough, mix together the salt, yeast and water in a jug Sift the flour into a large bowl, make a well in the centre and add the yeast mixture along with the olive oil. Use a wooden spoon to mix everything together to create a wet dough.

Turn out the dough onto a clean well-floured surface and work it with your hands for about 5 minutes or until smooth and elastic. Shape into six balls, place on a tray and cover with a tea-towel. Leave in a warm place to rest for at least 30 minutes or until the dough nearly doubles in size.

Preheat the oven to 220°C/425°F/gas mark 7.

Once rested turn out the dough balls onto a floured surface. Use your hands (or a rolling pin) to push out from the centre to create six round discs, about 15cm in diameter. Place the pizza bases on oiled baking trays.

To prepare the vegetarian filling, mix all the ingredients in a large bowl, season and divide equally between three pizza bases, placing the filling on one half of each disc.

To prepare the meat filling, spread the pesto equally on the other three bases, and top with a slice of ham, two slices of mozzarella, a pinch of salt and pepper then cover with the remaining ham. Again, ensure that you place the filling on one half of each disc.

Gently fold the pizza discs over the filling, creating a half-moon shape and seal the edges carefully.

Cook in the middle of the oven for about 20 minutes or until golden brown. Rest the calzone on a wire rack for about a minute, then enjoy with a cold beer.

Roma is known for three important things: the Vatican, the Colosseum and this fantastic recipe. Usually gnocchi is made with flour and potato, but the Romans like to use semolina. I know that not many people like semolina or polenta but, believe you me, this will surprise you because the flavours are amazing. A great dish to prepare in the morning, ready to be cooked just before your guests arrive. You can use Parmesan instead of Pecorino.

Roman-style Semolina Gnocchi with Tomato and Basil Sauce

Gnocchi alla Romana SERVES 6

550ml full-fat milk

¼ nutmeg, freshly grated

300g coarse semolina

150g salted butter

200g freshly grated Pecorino Romano

4 eggs, beaten

FOR THE SAUCE

6 tablespoons olive oil

1 large onion, finely sliced

3 x 400g tins chopped tomatoes

15 basil leaves

Salt and freshly ground black pepper

Preheat the oven to 200°C/400°F/gas mark 6.

Put 550ml water, the milk and nutmeg in a large saucepan and bring to the boil. Sprinkle the semolina into the pan using one hand while whisking constantly with the other hand to prevent lumps forming. Whisk until the mixture begins to thicken. Change the whisk for a wooden spoon and cook over a medium heat for about 10 minutes, stirring constantly. The mixture is ready when it starts to come away from the sides of the pan.

Remove from the heat and mix in a third of the butter, half the cheese and the eggs. Season with salt and pepper.

Lightly dampen your worksurface with cold water and, using a metal spatula, spread the semolina until it is about 2cm thick. Allow to cool and firm up.

Once the semolina is firm, use a 5cm diameter pastry cutter to cut the semolina into even-sized circles.

Use some of the remaining butter to grease a shallow ovenproof serving dish. Arrange a layer of scraps from the leftover semolina on the base of the dish. Lay the semolina circles on top, overlapping.

Sprinkle the remaining cheese on top and dot with little knobs of the remaining butter. Grind over some black pepper and cook in the middle of the oven for about 25 minutes until golden and bubbling.

Meanwhile, make the sauce. Heat the olive oil in a large saucepan over a medium heat and gently fry the onion until softened. Add the chopped tomatoes and basil and season with salt and pepper.

Allow to simmer for 20 minutes, uncovered, stirring occasionally.

Once the gnocchi are cooked, pour some of the sauce in the middle of a serving dish, scoop over the gnocchi and serve immediately.

In my family, everybody loves chorizo especially when fried with beans and rocket leaves. So one day I went to buy some fresh squid and came up with this beautiful salad which is now one of our favourites whenever we have people to dinner. The sweetness of the squid with the spiciness of the chorizo is a perfect match. My only tip is to make sure that you dress the rocket leaves at the last minute, otherwise the leaves will discolour and get soggy.

Squid and Chorizo Salad with Beans and Rocket Leaves

Insalata di Calamari con Fagioli e Chorizo SERVES 6

100g tinned chick peas, drained

100g tinned borlotti beans, drained

15 cherry tomatoes, quartered

1 medium-hot red chilli, deseeded and thinly sliced

1 garlic clove, finely chopped

3 tablespoons chopped fresh flat-leaf parsley

2 tablespoons freshly squeezed lemon juice

8 tablespoons extra virgin olive oil

400g medium squid

80g hot chorizo sausage, cut into thin rounds

50g rocket leaves

Salt to taste

Place the chick peas and beans in a large bowl with the tomatoes, the chilli, garlic and parsley. Add the lemon juice with 5 tablespoons of the oil, season with salt and toss together.

To prepare the squid, pull the head and tentacles from the body pouch. (Work over a bowl or the sink to catch any ink.) Cut off and reserve the tentacles. Remove the beak from the head and discard the intestines. Pull out and discard the quill from inside the body pouch and wash the pouch, inside and out. Cut open the body pouch of each squid along one side and score the inside with the tip of a small sharp knife into a fine diamond pattern. Then cut each pouch first in half lengthways and then across to give you 7cm pieces.

Heat the remaining oil in a large frying pan over a high heat. Add the reserved tentacles and the squid pieces, scored side upwards, which means they will curl attractively. Sear for about 30 seconds, then turn over the pieces and continue to sear for a further 30 seconds until golden and caramelised. Season with salt, add the chorizo and cook for a further minute, still over a high heat.

Toss the rocket leaves through the bean salad and transfer to a large serving plate. Top with the squid and chorizo and serve immediately.

The last three summers I have spent my holiday on the island of Sardinia on the Costa Smeralda where I learned this wonderful recipe. Sardinia is famous for the production of saffron and I think that it works perfectly with skate. Use this dish to start a great dinner party and make sure that you serve a good bottle of Italian white wine with it.

Skate with Hot Tomato, Saffron and Caper Dressing

Razza alla Sarda SERVES 4

90ml extra virgin olive oil

½ teaspoon dried crushed chillies

5 garlic cloves, finely sliced

400g tinned plum tomatoes

Pinch of saffron strands

15g sultanas

2 x 250g skate wings, skinned and trimmed

Salt and freshly ground black pepper

TO SERVE

2 tablespoons small capers in brine, drained and rinsed

16 purple basil leaves

Put the oil in a medium saucepan over a medium heat. Add the chillies and garlic and, as soon they start to sizzle, add the tomatoes, saffron and sultanas. Season with salt.

Cook gently, uncovered, for about 30 minutes stirring occasionally with a wooden spoon to allow the tomatoes to break down.

Meanwhile, bring about 2 litres water to the boil in a large shallow pan. Stir in 1 tablespoon of salt.

Place the skate wings in the boiling salted water and gently simmer for 15 minutes.

Use a fish slice to lift the skate wings out of the water and transfer to a chopping board. Cut each wing into 2 pieces using a sharp knife.

To serve, divide half of the sauce between 4 serving plates, top each one with a piece of skate and spoon the remaining sauce down the centre of the skate.

Scatter with the capers, garnish with the purple basil and serve immediately.

What a great vegetarian dish – full of colours, flavours and, of course, most importantly, simple to prepare. I often make this dish when I'm not sure if my guests are vegetarian or not, because I know that even a committed meat eater will like it. You can substitute the ricotta cheese with a good cottage cheese and, if you don't like rosemary, you can always use fresh thyme or chives instead.

Stuffed Red Pimentos with Ricotta, Rosemary and Chilli Olive Oil

Diavoletti Ripieni SERVES 8

10 long thin red pimento peppers

2 tablespoons olive oil

1 tablespoon salted capers, rinsed under cold water and drained

250g ricotta cheese

1 tablespoon fresh rosemary leaves, stripped from the stalks, finely chopped

Juice of 1 small lemon

Chilli-flavoured olive oil, for drizzling

Salt and freshly ground black pepper

Place the peppers on a chopping board and use a sharp medium knife to cut them lengthways and remove the seeds.

Place the peppers in a large bowl, drizzle with olive oil and season with salt and pepper. Toss well.

Heat a griddle pan until very hot and cook the peppers until lightly charred on both sides.

Meanwhile, finely chop the capers and place in a bowl with the ricotta, rosemary and lemon juice. Season with a little salt.

While the peppers are still warm, use a teaspoon to spread the ricotta mixture into the cut sides.

Place the stuffed peppers on a large serving dish, drizzle with chilli olive oil and serve warm as a starter or to accompany your favourite fish dish.

I'm not a big fan of coriander, ginger or dates. One day I was challenged by a friend to come up with a recipe with these three ingredients that I would serve at a dinner party. To be honest with you, I had a nightmarish two days trying to come up with something that I would enjoy. Then I remembered a great Moroccan recipe that I learned when I was working in Marbella. I know that it may sound cheeky, but I call this an Italian lamb tagine.

Italian Lamb Tagine

Stufato di Agnello alla Marocchina SERVES 8

1.5kg boned leg of lamb, cut into 4cm cubes

1 teaspoon ground ginger

⅛ teaspoon saffron strands

1 teaspoon ground coriander

4 tablespoons extra virgin olive oil

300g shallots, unpeeled

1 tablespoon plain flour

2 tablespoons tomato purée

150g pitted Kalamata olives

500ml chicken stock

3 tablespoons chopped fresh flat-leaf parsley

1 cinnamon stick

80g stoned dates

2 tablespoons runny honey

Salt and freshly ground black pepper

Place the lamb in a large bowl with the ginger, saffron and coriander. Drizzle with 1 tablespoon of oil, mix well, cover with clingfilm and refrigerate for 6 hours or overnight.

Bring a medium saucepan of water to the boil. Cook the shallots for 2 minutes, drain, refresh in cold water and peel.

When the meat has marinated, preheat the oven to 180°C/350°F/ gas mark 4.

Heat the remaining oil in a heavy-based ovenproof casserole. Add the lamb and start to brown the pieces for about 5 minutes.

Stir in the flour with the tomato purée and continue to cook for a further 2 minutes, stirring continuously. Add the shallots, olives, stock, parsley and the cinnamon stick. Season with salt and pepper, mix and bring to the boil.

Cover the casserole with a lid and transfer to the oven. Cook for 1½ hours, stirring occasionally, then remove the cinnamon stick and add the dates and honey. Stir to mix and return to the oven for a further 20 minutes.

Serve hot with a beautiful lemon couscous (see page 83).

For anyone who loves turkey but is bored with the traditional ways of cooking it, you have just found the recipe that you need. In my house we have saltimbocca at least once a week because it's easy to prepare and most importantly full of flavour. You can definitely try it with chicken breasts and, if you don't like Parma ham, use pancetta. In the event that you don't have Marsala wine, a good brandy can also be used.

Turkey Saltimbocca with Sage and Parma Ham

Saltimbocca di Tacchino SERVES 4

4 medium turkey breasts

4 slices Parma ham, cut in half widthways

16 small fresh sage leaves

3 tablespoons olive oil

50g salted butter

180ml Marsala

Salt and freshly ground black pepper

Place the turkey breasts on a chopping board and cover with clingfilm. Use a meat mallet to bash out each breast until flattened.

Cut the breasts in half widthways to give you 8 pieces in total. Season with a little salt and pepper and lay a piece of Parma ham on each breast. Top with 2 sage leaves and secure with a cocktail stick.

Heat the oil and half of the butter in a large frying pan over a medium heat. Once hot, place the saltimbocca in the pan, ham side down. Cook for 2 minutes until browned. Turn over and cook for a further 3 minutes until just cooked through.

Once ready, transfer the saltimbocca onto a plate and cover with foil.

Pour the Marsala wine into the hot frying pan and use a wooden spoon to deglaze the pan by scraping up the meaty bits on the bottom. Simmer over a high heat for 2 minutes until the sauce is slightly reduced. Stir in the remaining butter and season.

Return the saltimbocca and any juices to the pan, turning them in the sauce for 30 seconds. Remove the pan from the heat and remove the cocktail sticks from the saltimbocca.

Serve 2 pieces of saltimbocca per person on warm serving plates and enjoy accompanied with Cheesy Mash (see page 125). Perfect with a glass of cold dry wine.

For anyone who loves burgers, this has to be the ultimate recipe. To me this is the perfect party food because you can prepare and cook the burgers in advance and just heat them up when needed. The relish too can also be prepared in advance, leaving you time to enjoy your guests rather than spending loads of time in the kitchen. I chose lamb because it gives the burgers a great texture but, if you want, you can try minced beef or pork.

Lamb Burgers with Spicy Tomato and Red Pepper Relish

Burgers di Agnello con Salsina Piccante SERVES 4

FOR THE BURGERS

500g minced lamb

½ red pepper, cored, deseeded and finely chopped

½ onion, finely chopped

½ teaspoon chilli powder

1 tablespoon tomato ketchup

4 tablespoons chopped fresh flat-leaf parsley

2 tablespoons extra virgin olive oil

Salt

FOR THE RELISH

1 tablespoon olive oil

½ onion, finely chopped

½ red pepper, cored, deseeded and finely chopped

1 ripe plum tomato, deseeded and diced

½ teaspoon sugar

½ teaspoon chilli powder

1 tablespoon red wine vinegar

2 tablespoons chopped fresh flat-leaf parsley

1 ciabatta loaf, halved lengthways

Place the minced meat in a large bowl with the red pepper, onion, chilli powder, ketchup and parsley. Season with salt and mix well until combined. Divide the mixture into four balls and shape each one into 3cm thick burgers.

To make the relish, heat the oil in a small frying pan. Add the onion, pepper, tomato, sugar, chilli powder and vinegar. Season with salt and cook over a medium heat for 3 minutes until thickened. Stir in the parsley and set aside to cool.

Heat the extra virgin olive oil in a large frying pan over a medium heat and cook the burgers for 6 minutes on each side for a medium burger or for 8 minutes on each side for well-done.

Meanwhile, place the ciabatta bread on a hot griddle pan and cook until golden and crispy on both sides.

Cut the griddled ciabatta pieces in half and arrange on warmed serving plates. Place a lamb burger on each one. Spoon the relish over the top and serve with a few salad leaves and a cold beer.

Many people are too frightened to cook pheasant because they believe that it is too complicated to prepare. Well, I will prove that this is not the case with this typical Northern Italian recipe that will leave your guests completely gobsmacked with the flavour and presentation. Please make sure that once the pheasant is cooked, you let it rest for a good ten minutes so it becomes tender. You can try this recipe with a large chicken, if you like.

The Ultimate Roast Pheasant with Yummy Vegetables

Fagiano al Forno con Vegetali SERVES 6

2 tablespoons fresh rosemary leaves, stripped from the stalks

2 tablespoons fresh thyme leaves, stripped from the sprigs

8 garlic cloves

1 pheasant, cut in half down the breastbone

3 carrots, unpeeled and cut into 3cm chunks

3 courgettes, cut into 3cm chunks

3 potatoes, peeled and cut into 4cm chunks

6 tablespoons extra virgin olive oil

Salt and freshly ground black pepper

Preheat the oven to 200°C/400°F/gas mark 6.

Finely chop the rosemary, thyme and garlic with a sharp knife.

Make several cuts in the skin of the pheasant and stuff the herb mixture into the cuts.

Place the prepared vegetables in a roasting tin, drizzle with half of the oil, season with salt and pepper and mix well.

Lay the pheasant on top of the vegetables, skin side up, drizzle with the remaining oil and roast in the middle of the oven for 35 minutes. After the first 15 minutes, baste the pheasant with the cooking juices from the bottom of the tin.

To check that the bird is cooked, pierce each half with a skewer; if the juices run clear, it is ready.

Remove the pheasant from the tin, cut each piece into three and replace on top of the vegetables. Roast for a further 5 minutes.

Remove from the oven and rest for 10 minutes to allow the meat to relax and become more tender.

To serve, place the vegetables and the pheasant on a large serving plate and enjoy with a beautiful bottle of Italian red wine.

When I was in Italy recently I visited the first restaurant that I worked in when I was a kid, which is called Franco. I had a chance to cook with the owner, Salvatore, and we came up with this beautiful fish recipe that since then has been one of my favourites at my dinner parties. You can substitute the salmon with trout or seabass and please make sure that you use good-quality ripe plum tomatoes.

Baked Whole Salmon with Roasted Tomatoes, Potatoes and Anchovies

Salmone alla Vesuviana SERVES 4

1kg potatoes, peeled and cut into 1cm slices

5 large plum tomatoes, quartered lengthways

2 red peppers, deseeded and cut into 8 chunks

2 yellow peppers, deseeded and cut into 8 chunks

60g anchovy fillets in oil, drained

160ml vegetable stock

6 garlic cloves, halved

4 sprigs fresh oregano

4 sprigs fresh rosemary

6 tablespoons extra virgin olive oil, plus extra for drizzling

1 whole salmon, weighing about 1.5kg, cleaned, head and tail on

Sea salt and freshly ground black pepper

Preheat the oven to 200°C/400°F/gas mark 6.

Bring the potatoes to the boil in a large saucepan of salted water and cook for 5 minutes. Drain and arrange the slices over the base of a roasting tin large enough to accommodate the whole salmon.

Scatter the tomatoes and peppers over the potatoes. Break the anchovy fillets over the vegetables and pour in the stock. Add the garlic, oregano and rosemary, and season with salt and pepper.

Pour over the oil and roast in the middle of the oven for 30 minutes.

Meanwhile, slash the salmon 5 times down both sides and then slash in the opposite direction on one side to create an attractive criss-cross pattern. Rub well with more extra virgin olive oil, season with salt and pepper and place the fish on top of the vegetables.

Return the tin to the oven and continue to roast for a further 35–40 minutes or until the salmon is cooked through.

Once ready, divide the fish between 4 serving plates accompanied with the roasted vegetables.

Buonissimo with a cold bottle of Italian dry white wine.

If I had to choose one recipe that will guarantee smiling faces in my house this will definitely be the one. My boys love spare ribs in any way I cook them, but this is their absolute favourite. I have tried this dish at many garden or indoor parties and it always works a treat. If you want, once marinated, you can easily cook the ribs on a barbecue, but please make sure that they are sticky and glossy.

Roasted Pork Spare Ribs with Maple Syrup and Rosemary

Scottadita allo Sciroppo di Acero SERVES 6

24 pork spare ribs

2 tablespoon olive oil

5 tablespoons maple syrup

1 tablespoon chopped fresh rosemary leaves, stripped from the stalks

2 tablespoons soy sauce

200ml apple juice

8 garlic cloves, unpeeled

Salt and freshly ground black pepper

Place the ribs in a large bowl, season with salt and pepper and add all the other ingredients.

Use your hands to massage the marinade into the ribs. Cover with clingfilm and leave to rest in the fridge for 15 hours. If you can, massage the ribs with the marinade every 3 hours or so.

Once ready, remove the bowl from the fridge. Preheat the oven to 200°C/400°F/gas mark 6.

Place the marinated ribs in a large roasting tin, cover with foil and cook in the middle of the oven for 15 minutes.

Remove the foil and continue to cook for a further 30 minutes.

Turn the ribs in the tray and continue to cook for a further 45 minutes until the ribs look sticky and glossy.

Place on a large serving platter and serve immediately.

This is a gorgeous dessert that needs very little effort to prepare, yet tastes wonderful and looks amazing. I don't think that I've ever met anyone yet who doesn't like Amaretti biscuits or Amaretto liqueur so I can guarantee you that everyone will enjoy this unique Italian half-frozen dessert. Make sure that you serve it as soon as it's sliced and placed on a serving plate – before it melts too much.

Ice-Cream Cake with Nougat and Amaretto

Semifreddo all'Amaretto SERVES 8

Oil for greasing

1 vanilla pod

4 large eggs, separated into 2 large clean dry bowls

50g caster sugar

500ml double cream

350g torrone (almond nougat)

3 tablespoons runny honey

10 hard Amaretti biscuits, crushed (use your hands)

5 tablespoons Amaretto liqueur

Icing sugar, for dusting

Oil a 1.5-litre, 7cm deep mould or loaf tin and line it with two layers of clingfilm.

Slit the vanilla pod lengthways, scrape out the seeds and place in the bowl with the egg yolks. (Don't waste the vanilla pod: place it in a jar of sugar to create beautiful vanilla-flavoured sugar.) Beat in the sugar for about 5 minutes using an electric whisk until the mixture is thick and pale.

Clean the whisk and whip the cream into soft peaks.

Clean the whisk again and whip the egg whites into stiff peaks.

Place the torrone in a plastic bag and smash it into small pieces using a rolling pin.

Gently fold the whipped cream, honey, biscuits and the nougat into the egg yolk mixture. Fold in the egg whites with the Amaretto liqueur and spoon the mixture into the prepared mould or loaf tin.

Cover the top of the mixture with clingfilm and place in the freezer to rest for at least 5 hours.

To serve, remove from the freezer and allow it to thaw slightly (about 3–5 minutes). Remove the clingfilm, turn out the cake and cut into 2-cm thick slices.

Place 2 slices on a serving plate, dust with a little icing sugar and serve with your favourite cup of coffee.

If you are a trifle lover and fancy something with a bit more of a kick, this is the recipe to try. Of course I had to put a bit of an Italian twist in, so I used Limoncello liqueur and mascarpone cheese. If you can't find Pandoro or Panettone, you can use a good-quality sponge cake instead and make sure that you use a glass serving dish so you can see the colourful layers in the trifle.

Limoncello Trifle

Zuppa Inglese al Limoncello SERVES 8

200g golden caster sugar

100ml Limoncello liqueur

300g blueberries

½ teaspoon arrowroot, mixed to a smooth paste with 2 tablespoons cold water

5 eggs, separated

250g mascarpone

6 heaped tablespoons lemon curd

1 Pandoro cake, cut into 2cm slices (or Panettone)

550ml double cream

Handful of toasted flaked almonds

Put half the sugar and 300ml water in a medium saucepan and dissolve over a medium heat. Cook for 5 minutes, stirring occasionally.

Measure off 80ml of the sugar syrup into a bowl, pour in the Limoncello, mix well and set aside to cool.

Add most of the blueberries to the pan with the remaining sugar syrup and cook over a medium heat for 2 minutes until they are beginning to release some of their juice. (Reserve a few for decoration.)

Stir the arrowroot paste into the pan with the blueberries and cook for a further minute, stirring continuously. Allow to cool.

Place the egg yolks and the remaining sugar in a large bowl and whisk until pale and thick. Beat in the mascarpone and the lemon curd.

In a separate clean dry bowl, whisk the egg whites until soft peaks form. Gently fold into the mascarpone and lemon curd mixture.

Place a layer of Pandoro in a large 1.5-litre glass serving bowl. Brush with a third of the Limoncello syrup, then spread with a third of the curd mixture. Top with a third of the berries and their syrup. Repeat the layers twice, brushing the cake with the remaining Limoncello syrup, and ensuring the top layer is the lemon curd mixture.

Cover the bowl with clingfilm and chill for 5 hours or overnight.

To serve, whip the cream to soft peaks and spread evenly over the trifle. Scatter with the reserved blueberries and toasted flaked almonds.

This is what I call a wow dessert. Don't be afraid of making the pavlova because if you try it my way it will always work. It's a fantastic dessert that can be served at a summer or winter party – the only difference would be to change the type of berries that you use. For maximum satisfaction, use Jersey cream for the topping and please use fresh basil and not the dried stuff that comes in jars.

Strawberry Pavlova with Basil, Lime and Balsamic Vinegar

Pavlova con Fragole e Aceto Balsamico SERVES 8

6 large egg whites

350g caster sugar (preferably from a jar in which you have buried a couple of vanilla pods)

1 teaspoon white wine vinegar

2 teaspoons cornflour

2 tablespoons finely chopped fresh basil

Zest of 1 lime and 1 teaspoon lime juice

FOR THE TOPPING

400g fresh strawberries, halved

3 tablespoons caster sugar (see left)

2 tablespoons finely chopped fresh basil plus 8 small basil leaves to decorate

2 teaspoons balsamic vinegar

250ml Jersey cream

150ml whipping cream

Few drops of vanilla extract

Line a baking sheet with non-stick baking parchment and draw a 25cm diameter circle on it. Preheat the oven to 180°C/350°F/gas mark 4.

Put the egg whites in a large clean dry bowl and whisk until stiff. The whisk should make a stiff peak when drawn out of the egg whites.

Whisk in half of the sugar and continue to whisk until the mixture is thick and glossy. Use a spatula to fold in the remaining sugar, then the vinegar, cornflour, basil, lime zest and juice.

Spoon the meringue on to the baking sheet, following the circle. Make a dip in the centre with the back of a spoon and create peaks at the edges.

Place in the middle of the oven and bake for 5 minutes. Reduce the temperature to 140°C/275°F/gas mark 1 and continue to cook for a further hour. Turn off the heat and leave the meringue in the oven for at least 5 hours or overnight.

Once the meringue is ready, place the strawberries in a bowl and toss with the sugar, chopped basil and balsamic vinegar. Leave to marinate for 1 hour, tossing occasionally.

About 30 minutes before serving, whip the creams together in a large bowl with the vanilla extract until soft peaks form. Pile the cream onto the meringue base.

Arrange the strawberries on top, using a slotted spoon.

Just before serving spoon over the juices and decorate with the small basil leaves.

SERVES
8

What a wonderful way to end a meal. Very impressive, very tasty, very colourful and very, very healthy. OK, maybe not that healthy, but come on, once in a while it has to be done. To make your life easier, you can prepare the raspberry sauce a couple of hours in advance and if you want, once the soufflés are ready, make a hole in the centre and pour in the sauce. This is a dessert to remember!

Hot Chocolate Soufflés with Raspberry and Grand Marnier Sauce

Soufflés al Cioccolato con Salsa di Lamponi SERVES 6

30g salted butter at room temperature, for greasing

300g dark chocolate (at least 70 per cent cocoa solids)

4 egg yolks

8 egg whites

120g caster sugar, plus extra for sprinkling

Icing sugar for dusting

FOR THE SAUCE

220g raspberries

70g icing sugar

50ml red wine

50ml Grand Marnier

Preheat the oven to 220°C/425°F/gas mark 7. Butter six individual ramekin dishes, sprinkle with a little caster sugar and shake out any excess. Chill until required.

Melt the chocolate in a heatproof bowl over a pan of simmering water. Make sure that the water doesn't touch the base of the bowl. Once the chocolate has melted, leave to cool slightly. Gently beat in the 4 egg yolks, one at a time, until the mixture thickens.

Whisk the egg whites in a large clean dry bowl until stiff. Whisk in the caster sugar, a tablespoon at a time.

Fold a little of the egg white mixture into the melted chocolate, then fold the chocolate mix into the remaining whisked egg whites until evenly combined.

Divide the soufflé mixture between the prepared ramekins. Run your finger between the inside edge of each ramekin and the mixture to make a small groove to help the soufflés to rise evenly.

Place the ramekins on a baking tray and bake in the middle of the oven for 12–14 minutes until well risen and just wobbly in the middle.

Meanwhile, make the sauce. Blitz the raspberries in a food processor then pass through a sieve into a small saucepan.

Add the icing sugar, wine and Grand Marnier. Bring to a simmer and cook for 5 minutes until slightly reduced, stirring occasionally.

Dust the soufflés with icing sugar and serve immediately with the warm sauce.

My late grandfather, nonno Giovanni, was renowned for this dessert. It was created by him about 35 years ago, when he used to have a restaurant on the island of Sardinia. Although I wasn't even born when this dish was created, I feel as if there is a special bond between us, as I would have picked exactly the same ingredients and cooked it exactly the same way. You can substitute the Grand Marnier with Limoncello liqueur.

Orange and Grand Marnier Upside Down Cake

Torta alle Arance e Grand Marnier SERVES 8

4 oranges, peeled and sliced into 5mm slices

3 large eggs

120g caster sugar

1 teaspoon baking powder

2 tablespoons grated orange zest

125g plain flour, sifted

210g granulated sugar

3 tablespoons Grand Marnier, to serve

Preheat the oven to 180°C/350°F/gas mark 4.

Make the caramel by combining the granulated sugar with 3 teaspoons water in a small non-stick pan. Place over a medium heat, stirring occasionally until dissolved. Once the sugar mixture is gently boiling and starting to darken, remove the pan from the heat and pour the caramel into the base of a 20cm flan dish.

Gently push the orange slices into the caramel, arranged slightly overlapping. Set aside.

Put the eggs in a large bowl and whisk until fluffy and nearly double in size. Tip in the caster sugar and continue to whisk until creamy and thick.

Add the baking powder and the orange zest and continue to whisk until the mixture forms thick ribbons. Gradually add the flour and fold it in carefully to retain as much air in the mixture as possible.

Pour the mixture into the flan dish over the orange slices and bake in the middle of the oven for 25 minutes. To test the cake is cooked insert a cocktail stick in the centre of the sponge and if it comes out clean the sponge is ready.

Remove the dish from the oven and use a knife to cut around the edge of the sponge.

Wearing oven gloves, place a serving plate over the top of the flan dish and quickly invert the plate and the tin to turn out the orange sponge. (Be careful as the caramel sauce will be very hot.)

Drizzle over the Grand Marnier and serve at room temperature with a good-quality vanilla ice cream.

Conversion chart

Weight (solids)

7g	¼oz
10g	½oz
20g	¾oz
25g	1oz
40g	1½oz
50g	2oz
60g	2½oz
75g	3oz
100g	3½oz
110g	4oz (¼lb)
125g	4½oz
150g	5½oz
175g	6oz
200g	7oz
225g	8oz (½lb)
250g	9oz
275g	10oz
300g	10½oz
310g	11oz
325g	11½oz
350g	12oz (¾lb)
375g	13oz
400g	14oz
425g	15oz
450g	1lb
500g (½kg)	18oz
600g	1¼lb
700g	1½lb
750g	1lb 10oz
900g	2lb
1kg	2¼lb
1.1kg	2½lb
1.2kg	2lb 12oz
1.3kg	3lb
1.5kg	3lb 5oz
1.6kg	3½lb
1.8kg	4lb
2kg	4lb 8oz
2.25kg	5lb
2.5kg	5lb 8oz
3kg	6lb 8oz

Volume (liquids)

5ml	1 teaspoon
10ml	1 dessertspoon
15ml	1 tablespoon or ½fl oz
30ml	1fl oz
40ml	1½fl oz
50ml	2fl oz
60ml	2½fl oz
75ml	3fl oz
100ml	3½fl oz
125ml	4fl oz
150ml	5fl oz (¼ pint)
160ml	5½fl oz
175ml	6fl oz
200ml	7fl oz
225ml	8fl oz
250ml (0.25 litre)	9fl oz
300ml	10fl oz (½ pint)
325ml	11fl oz
350ml	12fl oz
370ml	13fl oz
400ml	14fl oz
425ml	15fl oz (¾ pint)
450ml	16fl oz
500ml (0.5 litre)	18fl oz
550ml	19fl oz
600ml	20fl oz (1 pint)
700ml	1¼ pints
850ml	1½ pints
1 litre	1¾ pints
1.2 litres	2 pints
1.5 litres	2½ pints
1.8 litres	3 pints
2 litres	3½ pints

Length

5mm	¼ inch
1cm	½ inch
2cm	¾ inch
2.5cm	1 inch
3cm	1¼ inches
4cm	1½ inches
5cm	2 inches
7.5 cm	3 inches
10cm	4 inches
15cm	6 inches
18cm	7 inches
20cm	8 inches
24cm	10 inches
28cm	11 inches
30 cm	12 inches

Oven temperatures

Celsius*	Farenheit	Gas	Description
110°C	225°F	Gas Mark ¼	cool
120°C	250°F	Gas Mark ½	cool
130°C	275°F	Gas Mark 1	very low
150°C	300°F	Gas Mark 2	very low
160°C	325°F	Gas Mark 3	low
180°C	350°F	Gas Mark 4	moderate
190°C	375°F	Gas Mark 5	mod. hot
200°C	400°F	Gas Mark 6	hot
220°C	425°F	Gas Mark 7	hot
230°C	450°F	Gas Mark 8	very hot
240°C	475°F	Gas Mark 9	very hot

* For fan-assisted ovens, reduce temperatures by 10°C

Temperature conversion
C=5/9 (F-32)
F=9/5C +32

Index

acknowledgements

Finally I've finished and, strangely enough, this time has been easier than the first time. I can proudly say I'm no longer a virgin author. Of course all this would have been impossible without the help of all my family, especially my wife, Jessie, and my two boys, Luciano and Rocco.

Once again, a big thank you to all the crew at Kyle Cathie, who trusted me to write a second book. A special thank you to Muna, Kate and Carl who put it all together so beautifully and for putting up with me.

A big kiss goes to Nicole for making sure that the food looked fantastic.

Grazie, grazie, grazie to everybody at Bontà Italia, once again, for supporting me — and eating all the food as I was trying out recipes.

To my friend, British father and agent, Mr Jeremy Hicks, who continues to believe in me and to whom I will be forever grateful for everything you do. (Don, I have to admit that this time it's really been full on!)

Finally, *grazie* to all of you for choosing my book — *Buon Appetito!*

This edition first published in Great Britain in 2013 by
Kyle Books
an imprint of Kyle Cathie Ltd.
67–69 Whitfield Street, London, WIT 4HF
general.enquiries@kylebooks.com
www.kylebooks.com

First published in Great Britain in 2008 by Kyle Cathie Ltd

10 9 8 7 6 5 4 3 2 1

978 0 85783 221 4

Text © 2008 Gino D'Acampo
Photography © 2008 Kate Whitaker
Book design © 2008 Kyle Books

Editorial Director Muna Reyal
Designer Carl Hodson
Photographer Kate Whitaker
Food Stylist Nicole Herft
Props Liz Belton
Copy Editor Stephanie Evans
Production Director Sha Huxtable

A Cataloguing In Publication record for this title is available from the British Library.

Colour reproduction by Chromagraphic
Printed and bound in China by C&C Offset Printing Company Ltd.